How to Learn Any Language

How to Learn Any Language

Quickly, Easily, and On Your Own!

Barry Farber

MJF BOOKS

NEW YORK

Published by MJF Books
Fine Communications
322 Eighth Avenue
New York, NY 10001

How to Learn Any Language
LC Control Number 2002104920
ISBN 1-56731-543-7

This edition published by arrangement with Citadel Press, a division of
Kensington Publishing Corp.

Manufactured in the United States of America on acid-free paper ∞

MJF Books and the MJF colophon are trademarks of Fine Creative Media,
Inc.

BG   10 9   8   7   6   5   4   3   2   1

To Bibi and Celia, for the pleasure of helping teach them their first language, followed by the pleasure of having them then teach me their second!

Contents

Acknowledgments

I want to thank my editor, Bruce Shostak, without whose skill and patience much of this book would have been intelligible only to others who've had a blinding passion for foreign languages since 1944. I further thank my publisher, Steven Schragis, for venturing into publishing territory heretofore officially listed as "uninteresting." Dr. Henry Urbanski, founder and head of the New Paltz Language Immersion Institute, was good enough to review key portions of the manuscript and offer toweringly helpful amendments. Dr. Urbanski's associate, Dr. Hans Weber, was supremely helpful in safeguarding against error.

I further wish to thank all my fellow language-lovers from around the world who interrupted their conversations at practice parties of the Language Club to serve as willing guinea pigs for my questions and experimentations in their native languages.

How to Learn Any Language

Introduction

This may be the most frequently told joke in the world—it's repeated every day in almost every language:

"What do you call a person who speaks two languages?"

"Bilingual."

"What do you call a person who speaks three languages?"

"Trilingual."

"What do you call a person who speaks four languages?"

"Quadrilingual."

"What do you call a person who speaks only one language?"

"An *American!*"

With your help this book can wipe that smile off the world's face.

The reason Americans have been such notoriously poor language-learners up to now is twofold:

1.   We've never really *had* to learn other peoples' languages before, and

2.   Almost all foreign-language instruction available to the average American has been until now (one hates to be cruel) *worthless.* "I took two years of high-school French and four

more years in college and I couldn't even order orange juice in Marseilles" is more than a self-effacing exaggeration. It's a fact, a shameful, culturally impoverishing, economically dangerous, self-defeating fact!

Modern commerce and communications have erased reason 1.

You and the method laid out in this book, working together, will erase reason 2.

It started for me when I learned that the Norwegian word for "squirrel" was *acorn*. It may have been spelled *ekorn,* but it was pronounced *acorn.* Then I learned that "Mickey Mouse" in Swedish is *Mussie Pigg.* Again, the Swedish spelling varied, but so what? As delights like those continued to come my way, I realized I was being locked tighter and tighter into the happy pursuit of language love and language learning.

My favorite music is the babble of strange tongues in the marketplace. No painting, no art, no photograph in the world can excite me as much as a printed page of text in a foreign language I can't read—yet!

I embraced foreign-language study as a hobby as a teenager in 1944. When I was inducted into the army in 1952, I was tested and qualified for work in fourteen different languages. Since then I've expanded my knowledge of those languages and taken up others. Whether fluently or fragmentally, I can now express myself in twenty-five languages.

That may sound like a boast, but it's really a confession. Having spent so many years with no other hobby, I should today be speaking every one of those languages much better than I do. If you're a beginner, you may be impressed to hear me order a meal in Chinese or discuss the Tito-Stalin split in Serbo-Croatian, but only I know how much time and effort I wasted over those years *thinking* I was doing the right thing to increase my command of those and other languages.

This book, then, does *not* present the tried-and-true formula I've been using since 1944. It presents the tried-and-true formula I'd use if I could go back to 1944 and start all over again!

Common sense tells us we can't have dessert before we finish the meal; we can't have a slim figure until we diet; we can't have strong muscles until we exercise; we won't have a fortune until we make it. So far common sense is right.

Common sense also tells us, however, that we can't enjoy communicating in a foreign language until we learn it. This means years of brain-benumbing conjugations, declensions, idioms, exceptions, subjunctives, and irregular verbs. And here common sense is wrong, completely wrong. When it comes to learning foreign languages, we can *start* with the dessert and then use its sweetness to inspire us to back up and devour the main course.

What six-year-old child ever heard of a conjugation? Wouldn't you love to be able to converse in a foreign language as well as all the children of that tongue who've not yet heard of grammar? No, we're not going to rise up as one throaty revolutionary mob, depose grammar, drag it out of the palace by the heels, and burn it in the main square. We're just going to put grammar in its place. Up to now, grammar has been used by our language educators to anesthetize us against progress. If it's grammar versus fun, we're going to minimize grammar and maximize fun. We're going to find more pleasant ways to absorb grammar.

Unfortunately, there are a lot more "self-improvement" books than there is self-improvement. Too many books whose titles are heavy with promise turn out to be all hat and no cattle—not enough take-home after you deduct the generalities and exhortations to "focus" and "visualize" your goals. Extracting usable advice from high-promising books can be like trying to nail custard pies to the side of a barn.

Mindful of that danger, I will not leave you with nothing but a pep talk. Follow the steps herein, and you *will* learn the language of your choice *quickly, easily, inexpensively, enjoyably,* and *on your own.*

And you'll have fun en route, though not nearly as much fun as you'll have once you get that language in working order and take it out to the firing range of the real world!

The System

The language-learning system detailed in this book is the result of my own continuous, laborious trial and error beginning in 1944. That which worked was kept, that which failed was dropped, that which was kept was improved. Technology undreamed of when I started studying languages, such as the audiocassette and the tape player small enough to carry while walking or jogging, was instantly and eagerly incorporated.

The system combines:

- THE MULTIPLE TRACK ATTACK: Go to the language department of any bookstore and you'll see language books, grammars, hard-cover and paperback workbooks, readers, dictionaries, flash cards, and handsomely bound courses on cassette. Each one of those products sits there on the shelf and says, "Hey, Bud. You want to learn this language? Here I am. Buy me!" I say, buy them all, or at least one of each! You may feel like you're taking four or five different courses in the same language simultaneously. That's good. A marvelous synergistic energy sets you soaring when all those tools are set together in symphony.
- HIDDEN MOMENTS: Dean Martin once chided a chorus girl, who was apathetically sipping her cocktail, by saying, "I spill more than you drink!" All of us "spill" enough minutes every day to learn a whole new language a year! Just as the Dutch steal land from the sea, you will learn to steal language-learning time, even from a life that seems completely filled or overflowing. What do you do, for example, while you're waiting for an elevator, standing in line at the bank, waiting for the person you're calling to answer the phone, holding the line, getting gas, waiting to be ushered from the waiting room into somebody's office, waiting for your date to arrive, waiting for anything at any time?

You will learn to mobilize these precious scraps of time you've never even been aware you've been wasting. Some of your most valuable study time will come in mini-lessons of fifteen, ten, and even five seconds throughout your normal (though now usually fruitful) day.

- HARRY LORAYNE'S MAGIC MEMORY AID: An ingenious memory system developed by memory master Harry Lorayne will help you glue a word to your recollection the instant you encounter it. What would you do right now if I gave you a hundred English words along with their foreign equivalents and told you to learn them? Chances are you would look at the first English word, then look at the foreign word, repeat it several times, then close your eyes and keep on repeating it, then cover up the foreign word, look only at the English and see if you could remember how to say it in the language you're learning, then go on to the next word, then the next, and the next, and then go back to the first to see if you remembered it, and so on through the list.

  Harry Lorayne's simple memory trick based on sound and association will make that rote attempt laughable. The words will take their place in your memory like ornaments securely hung on a Christmas tree, one right after the other all the way up to many times those hundred words.

- THE PLUNGE: You will escape the textbook incubator early and leap straightaway, with almost no knowledge of the language, into that language's "real world." A textbook in your target language, no matter how advanced, is not the real world. On the other hand, an advertisement in a foreign-language magazine, no matter how elementary and easy to read, *is* the real world. Everything about you, conscious and subconscious, prefers real-world to student-world contact with the language.

  An actor knows the difference between rehearsal and opening night; the football player, between practice scrimmages and the kickoff in a crowded stadium. And you will know the difference between your lessons in the target language and the real-world newspapers, magazines, novels, movies, radio, TV, and anything else you can find to throw yourself into at a stage your high-school French teacher would have considered horrifyingly early!

There you have it: The Multiple-Track Attack, Hidden Moments, Harry Lorayne's Magic Memory Aid, The Plunge. Visualize the target language as a huge piece of thin, dry paper. This system will strike a match underneath the middle of that paper, and your knowledge, like the flame, will eat its way unevenly but unerringly outward to the very ends.

Just as food manufacturers like to label their products "natural and organic" whenever they can get away with it, many language courses like to promise that you will learn "the way a child learns."

Why bother? Why *should* you learn another language the way a child learned his first one? Why not learn as what you are—an adult with at least one language in hand, eager to use that advantage to learn the next language in less time than it took to learn the first?

PART ONE

My Story

A Life of Language Learning

A brief "language autobiography" may help readers whose language-learning and language-loving careers began only a few moments ago with the opening of this book.

My favorite word—in any language—is the English word *foreign.* I remember how it came to be my favorite word. At the age of four I attended a summer day camp. Royalty develops even among children that young. There were already a camp "king" and a camp "queen," Arthur and Janet. I was sitting right beside Arthur on the bus one morning, and I remember feeling honored. Arthur reached into his little bag, pulled out an envelope, and began to show Janet the most fascinating pieces of colored paper I'd ever seen.

"Look at these stamps, Janet," he said. "They're *foreign!*" That word reverberated through my bone marrow. *Foreign,* I figured, must mean beautiful, magnetic, impressive—something only the finest people share with only the other finest people. From that moment forward, the mere mention of the word *foreign* has flooded me with fantasy.

I thought everybody else felt the same, and I had a hard time realizing they didn't. When a schoolmate told me he turned down his parents' offer of a trip to Europe for a trip out West instead, I thought he was crazy. When another told me he found local politics more interesting than world politics, I thought he was nuts. Most kids are bored with their parents' friends who come to dinner. I was too, unless that friend happened to have been to a foreign country—*any* foreign country—in which case I cross-examined him ruthlessly on every detail of his foreign visit.

Once a visitor who'd been through my interrogation to the point of brain-blur said to my mother upon leaving, "What a kid! He was fascinated by every detail of every hour I ever spent in another country, *and the only other place I've ever been is Canada!"*

How Latin Almost Ruined It

Walking into Miss Leslie's Latin class on the first day of ninth grade was the culmination of a lifelong dream. I could actually hear Roman background music in my mind. I didn't understand how the other students could be anything less than enthusiastic about the prospect of beginning Latin. Electricity coursed through me as I opened the Latin book Miss Leslie gave us. I was finally *studying a foreign language!*

The first day all we did was learn vocabulary. Miss Leslie wrote some Latin words on the blackboard, and we wrote them down in our notebooks. I showed early promise as the class whiz. I quickly mastered those new words, each then as precious as Arthur's foreign stamps had been eleven years earlier. When Miss Leslie had us close our books and then asked, "Who remembers how to say 'farmer' in Latin," I was the first to split the air with the cry of *"Agricola!"* I soaked up those foreign words like the Arabian desert soaks up spilled lemonade.

What happened thereupon for a short time crippled, but then enriched, my life beyond measure.

I was absent from school on day four. When I returned on day five, there were no more Latin words on the blackboard.

In their place were words like *nominative, genitive, dative, accusative*. I didn't know what those words meant and I didn't like them. That "nominative-genitive" whatever-it-was was keeping me from my feast, and I resented it like I resent the clergyman at the banquet whose invocation lasts too long.

The more Miss Leslie talked about those grammatical terms, the more bored I got. Honeymooners would have more patience with a life-insurance salesman who knocked on their motel door at midnight than I had with Latin grammar. I clearly remember believing languages were nothing but words. We have words. They have words. And all you have to do is learn their words for our words and you've got it made. Therefore all that "ablative absolute" stuff Miss Leslie was getting increasingly excited about was unneeded and, to me, unwanted.

Miss Leslie, noting that I, her highly motivated superstar, was floundering with elementary Latin grammar, kindly offered to assign another student to tutor me on what I'd missed the day before, or even to sit down with me herself. I remember declining the offer. I remember deciding, with the logic of a frustrated fifteen-year-old, that grammar was just another of those barriers designed by grown-ups to keep kids from having too much fun. I decided to wait it out.

I shut off my brain as the cascade of changing noun endings and mutating verb forms muscled out the joy of my beloved vocabulary words. I longed for the good old days of being the first in the class to know *agricola*. More and more that Miss Leslie said made less and less sense. I was trapped in a Bermuda Triangle. My aura of classroom celebrity disappeared, along with my self-esteem, my motivation, and almost my affection for things foreign.

I limped along, barely making passing grades; I only managed to pass thanks to the vocabulary section on every test. My knowledge of vocabulary plus some good grammatical guesswork and a little luck got me through Miss Leslie's class with a low D.

Some of the other students seemed to be enjoying my lameness in Latin, after my having been the overpraised and preening star of the class for the first three days. To assuage the hurt, I got hold of a self-study book in Chinese. By the last few weeks of school, it was apparent that there was no way I could make better than a weak D in Latin, but that was enough to pass. I hid my humiliation behind that outrageously foreign-looking book with thick, black Chinese characters all over the cover. I buried all thoughts of Latin in sour grapes and sat there and studied Chinese instead!

Chinese Sailors Don't Speak Latin

Forsaking Latin for Chinese was my own form of juvenile defiance. However, I have since used Chinese in some way almost every day. I confess to occasional curiosity as to what all those A students from Miss Leslie's Latin class are doing these days with their Latin.

During summer vacation we went to Miami Beach to visit my grandparents. On one trip, as Uncle Bill drove us from the train station in Miami to Miami Beach, we passed a large group of marching sailors. As we drew abreast of the last row I noticed that the sailor on the end was Chinese. Then I noticed that the sailor beside him was also Chinese. I blinked. That whole last row was Chinese. And the *next* whole row was Chinese too.

That entire contingent of marching sailors was Chinese!

I felt like a multimillion-dollar lottery winner slowly realizing he'd gotten all the right numbers. I had no idea there were Chinese sailors in Miami, but why not? It was during World War II, China was our ally, and Miami was a port. There they were, hundreds of native speakers of the language I was trying to learn.

I couldn't wait to fling myself into their midst sputtering my few phrases of Chinese at machine-gun velocity. I didn't know what adventures were awaiting my Latin classmates that summer, but I was confident none of them was about to approach an entire contingent of sailors who spoke Latin!

When we got to my grandparents' hotel, I gave them the quickest possible hug and kiss, ran out, took the jitney back over the causeway to Miami, and started asking strangers if they knew where the Chinese sailors were.

Everybody knew the Chinese sailors were billeted in the old Hotel Alcazar on Biscayne Boulevard. After their training, I was told, they gathered in groups and strolled around Bayfront Park.

I waited. Sure enough, in late afternoon the park filled with Chinese sailors. I picked a clump of them at random and waded on in, greeting them in phrases I'd been able to learn from the book my parents had bought me. I'd never heard Chinese spoken before. No records, tapes, or cassettes. I could hit them only with the Chinese a D student in Latin could assemble from an elementary self-study book in Chinese conversation in Greensboro, North Carolina.

It sounded extraplanetary to the Chinese sailors, but at least they understood enough to get the point that here was no Chinese-American, here was no child of missionary parents who'd served in China. Here was essentially an American urchin hellbent on learning Chinese without any help.

They decided to provide the help.

You don't have to win a war to get a hero's welcome. The Chinese naval units stationed in Miami seemed suddenly to have two missions—to defeat the Japanese and to help me learn Chinese! A great side benefit to learning foreign languages is the love and respect you get from native speakers when you set out to learn their language. You're far from an annoying foreigner to them. They spring to you with joy and gratitude.

The sailors adopted me as their mascot. We met every afternoon in Bayfront Park for my daily immersion in conversational Chinese. A young teenager surrounded by native speakers and eager to avenge a knockout by a language like Latin learns quickly. There was something eerie about my rapid progress. I couldn't believe I was actually speaking Chinese with our military allies in the shadow of the American-built destroyers on which they would return to fight in the Far East. If only Miss Leslie could see me now!

Naturally my grandparents were disappointed that I didn't spend much time with them, but their bitterness was more than assuaged when I brought gangs of my Chinese sailor friends over to Miami Beach and introduced them to my family. My grandparents had the pleasure of introducing me to their friends as "my grandson, the interpreter for the Chinese navy."

I exchanged addresses and correspondence with my main Chinese mentor, Fan Tung-shi, for the next five years. Sadly, his letters stopped coming when the Chinese Communists completed their conquest of the Mainland. (He and I were joyously reunited exactly forty years later when a Taiwan newspaper interviewed me and asked me how I learned Chinese. One of Fan's friends saw his name in the article.)

That summer, in Will's Bookstore on South Green Street back in Greensboro, I walked past the foreign-language section and spotted a book entitled *Hugo's Italian Simplified*. I opened it, and within ten or fifteen seconds the "background music" started again.

Arrivederci, *Latin*

Italian, I discovered, was Latin with all the difficulty removed. Much as a skilled chef filets the whole skeleton out of a fish, some friendly folks somewhere had lifted all that grammar (at least, most of it) out of Latin and called the remainder Italian!

There was no nominative-genitive-dative-accusative in Italian. Not a trace, except in a few pronouns which I knew I could easily take prisoner because we had the same thing in English (*me* is the accusative of *I*). Italian verbs did misbehave a little, but not to the psychedelic extent of Latin verbs. And Italian verbs were a lot easier to look at.

I bought Hugo's book and went through it like a hot knife through butter. I could have conversed in Italian within a month if there'd been anybody around who could have understood—a learning aid which the Greensboro of that day, alas, could not provide.

I was clearly a beaten boxer on the comeback trail. Why was I all of a sudden doing so well in Italian after having done so poorly in Latin?

Was it my almost abnormal motivation? No. I'd had that in Latin, too. Was it that Italian was a *living* language you could go someplace someday and actually speak, whereas Latin was something you could only hope to go on studying? That's a little closer to the mark, but far from the real answer.

My blitz through Italian, after my unsuccessful siege of Latin, owed much to the fact that in Italian *I didn't miss day four!* I'm convinced that it was day four in ninth-grade Latin that did me in. No other day's absence would have derailed me. When I left on day three we were bathing in a warm sea of pleasant words. If only I'd been there on day four when Miss Leslie explained the importance of grammar, I might have felt a bit dampened, but I'd have put my head into the book, clapped my hands over my ears, and mastered it.

After Italian I surged simultaneously into Spanish and French with self-study books. Though by no means fluent in either Spanish or French by summer's end, I had amassed an impressive payload of each. I was ready to stage my come-from-behind coup.

Regulations in my high school demanded that a student complete two years of Latin with good grades before continuing with another language. After that, one could choose Spanish or French. I had completed only *one* year of Latin with *poor* grades, and I wanted to take *both* Spanish *and* French!

I had not yet learned the apt Spanish proverb that tells us "regulations are for your enemies." I learned the concept, however, by living it.

Miss Mitchell was the sole foreign-language authority of the high school. She taught Spanish and French. She was considered unbendable—in fact, unapproachable—in matters of regulation-fudging. I didn't know that on the first day as classes were forming. I'm glad I didn't.

I went to her classroom and asked if I might talk something over with her. I told her I was particularly interested in foreign languages, and even though I'd only had one year of Latin and didn't do well in it at all, I'd really like to move into Spanish and French. If she could only see her way clear to let me, I'd appreciate it forever and try awfully hard.

She asked if I had a transcript of my grades from Miss Leslie's Latin class. No, I didn't, I explained, but I had something more to the point. I'd bought books in Spanish and French over the summer and gotten a good head start. I hoped a demonstration of my zeal would win her favor.

Like a tough agent softening sufficiently to let a persistent unknown comic do part of his routine, Miss Mitchell invited me to do my stuff.

I conversed, I read, I wrote, I recited, I conjugated, I even *sang*—first in Spanish, then in French. Miss Mitchell gave no outward sign of emotion, but I knew the magic had worked.

"I'll have to talk it over with the principal," she said, "but I don't think there will be a problem. We've never had a case anything like this before. If I can get approval, which language, Spanish or French, would you like to take?"

In a fit of negotiatory skill I wish would visit me more often, I said, "Please, Miss Mitchell, let me take both!"

She frowned, but then relented. I got to take both.

From the ambitious boxer floored early in round one by Latin grammar, I was all of a sudden the heavyweight language champ of the whole high school!

Ingrid Bergman Made Me Learn Norwegian

I did well in high-school Spanish and French. When you've pumped heavy iron, lifting a salad fork seems easy. When you're thrown into a grammar as complex as Latin's at the age of fourteen, just about any other language seems easy. I never quit thanking Spanish, French, German, Italian, Norwegian, Danish, Swedish, Romanian, and Yiddish just for not being Latin. I've always been particularly grateful to Chinese and Indonesian for having nothing in their entire languages a Latin student would recognize as grammar.

It was so enjoyable building my knowledge of Spanish, French, Italian, and Chinese, I never thought of taking on any other languages. Then I saw an Ingrid Bergman movie and came out in a daze. I'd never imagined a woman could be that attractive. I went directly to the adjoining bookstore and told the clerk, "I want a book in whatever language it is *she* speaks."

Miss Bergman's native tongue, the clerk told me, was Swedish, and he brought forth a copy of *Hugo's Swedish Simplified*. It cost two dollars and fifty cents. I only had two dollars with me.

"Do you have anything similar—cheaper?" I asked.

He did indeed. He produced a volume entitled *Hugo's Norwegian Simplified* for only one dollar and fifty cents.

"Will *she* understand if I speak to her in *this?*" I asked, pointing to the less-expensive Norwegian text. The clerk assured me that yes, any American speaking Norwegian would be understood by any native Swede.

He was right. A lifetime later, at age thirty, I wheedled an exclusive radio interview with Ingrid Bergman on the strength of my ability in her language. She was delighted when I told her the story. Or at least she was a nice enough person and a good enough actress to pretend.

Rumors of Russian

When I arrived at the University of North Carolina, I got my first real opportunity to speak the European languages I was learning with native speakers. Students at the university came from many different countries. The Cosmopolitan Club, a group of foreign students and Americans who wanted to meet one another, gathered every Sunday afternoon in the activities building. I felt like a bee flitting from blossom to blossom until it is too heavy with pollen to fly or even buzz.

A rumor rippled across the campus in my senior year that seemed too good to be true. The university, it was whispered, was planning to start a class in Russian.

Sure enough, the rumor was soon confirmed. It was a historic event. Not only was the course the first in Russian ever offered by the University of North Carolina (or possibly by any university in the South), it also represented the first time the university had offered what one student called a "funny-looking" language of any kind (he meant languages that don't use the Roman alphabet)!

The enrollment requirements were stiff. First you had to have completed at least two years in a "normal" language (Spanish, French, Italian, Portuguese) with good grades. I qualified and was accepted.

For me the first day of Russian was a lot like the first day of school. I'd toyed with one funny-looking language already (Chinese), but I knew Russian was a different kind of funny-looking. Would I conquer it, as I had Spanish and Norwegian, or would Russian swallow me whole, as Latin had?

There were forty-five of us in that Russian class thinking varying versions of the same thing when the teacher, a rangy Alabaman named "Tiger" Titus, entered the room. After a formal "Good morning" he went straight to the front of the room and wrote the Russian (Cyrillic) alphabet on the blackboard.

You could feel the group's spirit sink notch by notch as each of Russian's "funny-looking" letters appeared. Students were allowed under university rules to abandon a course and get themselves into another as long as they did it within three days after the beginning of the term. We had defections from Russian class in mid-alphabet. By the time Tiger Titus turned around to face us, he had fewer students than when he had entered the room.

"My soul!" exclaimed one of the deserters when I caught up with him in the cafeteria later that day. "I've never seen anything like that Russian alphabet before in my life. Why, they got *v*'s that look like *b*'s, *n*'s that look like *h*'s, *u*'s that look like *y*'s, *r*'s that look like *p*'s, and *p*'s that look like sawed-off goalposts. They got a backwards *n* that's really an *e* and an *x* that sounds like you're gagging on a bone. They got a vowel that looks like the number sixty-one, a consonant that looks like a butterfly with its wings all the way out, and damned if they don't even have a B-flat!"

The next day there were no longer forty-five members of the university's first Russian class. There were five.

I was one of the intrepid who hung in.

A Lucky Bounce to the Balkans

Writer-columnist Robert Ruark, a talented North Carolinian and drinking buddy of Ava Gardner, once wrote boastfully about a college weekend that began someplace like Philadelphia and got out of hand and wound up in Montreal. I topped him. I went to a college football game right outside Washington, D.C., one weekend and wound up in Yugoslavia for six weeks!

The previous summer I'd been named a delegate from the university to the national convention of the National Student Association. I came back as chairman for the Virginia-Carolinas region of NSA. In October I was in College Park, Maryland, for the Carolina-Maryland game. At half time, at the hot dog stand, who should be reaching for the same mustard-squirter as I but National NSA president, Bill Dentzer.

"Who can believe this?" he said. "We've been looking for you for three days!"

I explained it was our big senior out-of-town football weekend and College Park, Maryland, was a long way from Chapel Hill, North Carolina, and there was a lot going on and I was sorry he couldn't reach me. "Why were you looking for me?" I asked.

"We wanted you to go represent us in Yugoslavia," he said. I told him I'd love to.

"It's too late now," he said. "The plane leaves Monday from New York, and it's already Saturday afternoon and the State Department's closed, so there's no way to get you a passport . . ."

"Bill," I interrupted, "I *have* a passport. I can easily get back to Chapel Hill and pick it up in time to fly from New York on Monday."

By Wednesday I was attending sessions of a spirited Tito-propaganda fiesta called the Zagreb Peace Conference and enjoying my first immersion in a language the mere mention of which impresses people even more than Chinese: Serbo-Croatian!

To my delight, I understood entire phrases of it from my university Russian. I became aware of "families" of foreign languages, something that doesn't occur automatically to Americans because English doesn't resemble its cousins very closely. It's something of a black sheep in the Germanic language family. They say the closest language to English is Dutch. Dutch is about as close to English as Betelgeuse is to Baltimore!

I'd noticed the summer before that Norwegian is usefully close to Swedish and Danish. Serbo-Croatian sounded to me like a jazzier, more "fun" kind of Russian. They use the Roman alphabet in western Yugoslavia, Croatia, and Slovenia, and in Serbia to the east they use the Cyrillic alphabet, with even more interesting letters in it than Russian uses.

Some of the mystique I'd always imputed to multilingual people began to fade. If you meet somebody who speaks, say, ten languages, your instinct is to be impressed to the tune of ten languages' worth. If, however, you later learn that six of those languages are Russian, Czech, Slovak, Serbo-Croatian, Polish, and Ukrainian—I'm not suggesting you dismiss him as illiterate, but you ought to be aware that he got six of those languages for the price of about two and three-fourths! They're all members of the Slavic family.

The Yugoslav university students, my hosts, sent me back home aboard a Yugoslav ship, leaving me sixteen days with nothing to do but practice Serbo-Croatian with the other passengers. When I got back to school after a solid eight-weeks' absence, I wasn't even behind in my German. German is widely spoken in central Europe and I'd spoken it widely enough during the adventure to float almost even with the class.

Exotics—Hard and Easy

Expertise is a narcotic. As knowledge grows, it throws off pleasure to its possessor, much like an interest-bearing account throws off money. A pathologist who can instantly spot the difference between normal and abnormal X-rays grows incapable of believing there are those of us who can't. I find it hard to believe there are Americans who can't even tell the difference between printed pages of Spanish and French or of Polish, Danish, or anything else written in the Roman alphabet. Too bad. If you can't distinguish the easier languages from the harder ones, you miss the higher joys of confronting your first samples of written Finnish.

Finland has been called the only beautiful country in the world where the language is the major tourist attraction. It's utterly unfamiliar to you no matter where you come from, unless you happen to come from Estonia, in which case Finnish is only half unfamiliar to you. There's always a general-knowledge heavyweight around who says, "Wait a minute. Finnish is related to Hungarian too!"

Oh, yeah! True, Finnish, Hungarian, and Estonian are indeed all members of the Finno-Ugric language family, but try to find more than six words even remotely similar in each. As you learn more and more about foreign languages, you're able to laugh at more and more jokes about languages. No Las Vegas comic will ever knock socks off, or even loosen them, by standing up and saying, "You know, Finnish and Hungarian are cousin languages, but Finnish took all the vowels!" Look at the two languages side by side, however, and you'll grudgingly accord at least minor-wit status to whoever thought that one up.

You may have experienced the difficulties of tackling Latin and Russian with their half-dozen or so noun cases. Finnish has fifteen noun cases in the singular and sixteen in the plural! Every word in the entire language is accented on the first syllable, which gives Finnish something of the sound of a pneumatic jackhammer breaking up a sidewalk.

I covered the Olympic games in Helsinki but wisely decided not to try to learn Finnish. It was the wisdom of the young boxer who's eager to get in there with the champ and trade punches, but who nonetheless summons up the cool to decline and wait until he's more prepared. I found a much softer opponent on the ship back to the United States.

A summer tradition that vanished after the 1950s with far too little poetic lamentation was the "student ship to Europe." They were almost always Dutch ships offering unbelievably low fares, hearty food, cramped but clean accommodations, cheap beer, and always a bearded guitar player who drew the crowd back to the ship's fantail after dinner and led the kids of ten or twelve nations in throaty renditions of "I've Been Working on the Railroads." The singing, the flirting, the joy of heading over or heading home, and especially the learning of all the other countries' "Railroads" in all the other languages made the summer student ship a delight unimaginable to today's jet-lagged young.

Boarding the ship in Rotterdam was a group of uniformed Dutch airmen about my age. They were all headed for the United States to take their jet fighter training at various American air bases, and we became old friends at once. There seemed to be dozens (I later realized hundreds) of Indonesian servants on board. After four hundred years of Dutch rule, Indonesia had won its independence from Holland only four years earlier. The thousands of Indonesians who chose to remain loyal to Holland had to go to Holland, and that meant that virtually the entire Dutch service class was Indonesian.

I was sitting on deck talking to one of the Dutch pilots, Hans van Haastert. He called one of the Indonesians over and said something to him in fluent Indonesian. My romance with Dutch would begin (in a very unusual way) a few years later, but my romance with Indonesian was born in the lightning and thunder of Hans ordering a beer from that deck chair.

If I had never been drawn to foreign languages earlier, that moment alone would have done it. To me at that time, it was the white-suited *bwana* speaking something pure "jungle" to one of this water carriers in any one of a hundred and eighteen safari movies I'd seen. It was Humphrey Bogart melting a glamorous woman's kneecaps with a burst of bush-talk she had no idea he even knew.

"Where did you learn *that?*" I asked. It turned out that Hans, like many of his Dutch confreres, had been born in Java of mixed parents. His Indonesian was just as good as his Dutch. "Will you teach me some?" I asked.

For the next eight days, until we were interrupted by the New York City skyline, Hans patiently taught me the Indonesian language. When we parted, I was able to converse with the Indonesian crewmen, just as Hans had that first day on deck. Lest this come across as a boast, let me hasten to point out that Indonesian is the easiest language in the world—no hedging, no "almost," no "among the easiest." In my experience, Indonesian is the easiest. The grammar is minimal, regular, and simple. Once I began to learn it, Indonesian didn't seem "jungle" anymore. The Indonesians obligingly use the Roman alphabet, and they get along with fewer letters of it than we do. And their tongue has an instant charm. The Indonesian word for "sun," *mata hari* (the famous female spy was known as the "sun" of Asia) literally means "eye of the day." When they make a singular noun plural in Indonesia, they merely say it twice. "Man," for example, is *orang*. "Men" is *orang orang*. And when they write it, they just write one *orang* and put a *2* after it, like an exponent in algebra (*Orang 2*). *Orang hutan,* the ape name pronounced by many Americans as if it were "orang-u-tang," is an Indonesian term meaning "man of the forest."

My Toughest Opponent

For the next four years I avoided taking up any new languages. I had nothing against any of them (except one). It was just that there were too many gaps in the tongues I'd already entertained and I wanted to plug them up.

The language I had something against was Hungarian. Before a summer weekend with army buddies in Rehoboth Beach, Delaware, I went to the post library and checked out an army phrase book in Hungarian to look at over the weekend. The introduction bluntly warned, "Hungarian is perhaps the hardest language in the world, and it is spoken by only about ten million people." I resolved I'd never get any closer to it.

Hungarian was the next language I studied.

When Hungary rebelled against Soviet oppression in 1956, I was invited by the U.S. Air Force to join a team of reporters covering Operation Safe Haven, the airlift of all the Hungarian refugees who were to receive asylum in the United States. That was far from enough to make me want to study Hungarian—yet.

Every child is treated to fantasies like Buck Rogers and his invincible ray gun, Superman, Batman, or, in my case, Jack Armstrong and his "mystery eye," a power imparted to him by a friendly Hindu who, merely by concentrating and holding his palms straight out, could stop every oncoming object from a fist to a bullet to a bull to an express train. By this time I began to note that similar powers—offensive and defensive—could unexpectedly and delightfully accompany the mastery of languages.

No Iron Curtains for Language

Many reporters got to the Hungarian border with Austria during the outpouring of refugees that followed the Soviet oppression of the Hungarian freedom fighters. They went to the Red

Cross shelters on the Austrian side, interviewed some refugees and relief workers, and went home. I was invited to join a secret team of volunteer international "commandos" who actually slipped into Hungary by night to ferry refugees across the border canal on a rubber raft.

The center of the refugee operation was the Austrian border village of Andau. I asked a local policeman in German where the refugee headquarters was. It was Christmas night. It was dark. It was cold. There were no tour-bus operators on the streets hawking tickets to the Hungarian border. He told me to go to Pieck's Inn. At Pieck's Inn the bartender said, "Room nineteen." The fact that I was getting all this in German without looking around for somebody who spoke English was a convenience, but that's not what I mean by the power of another language. That came next.

I went upstairs to room nineteen and knocked on the door. "Who's there?" shouted a voice in interestingly accented English.

"I'm an American newspaper reporter," I yelled back. "I understand you might help me get to the Hungarian border."

He opened the door cussing. "I'll never take another American to the border with us again," he said before the door even opened. "No more Americans! One of you bastards damned near got us all captured night before last."

He turned out to be a pleasant-looking young man with blond hair. When I knocked, he was busy adjusting heavy-duty combat boots. He continued his tirade as we faced each other. "That American knew damned good and well that flashlights, flashbulbs, even matches were forbidden." He went on in rougher language than I'll here repeat to tell how an American with a camera broke his promise and popped off a flashbulb while a raft-load of refugees was in the middle of the canal, causing the refugees and the rescuers on both sides of the canal to scatter. That burst of light, of course, let the Communists know exactly where the escape operation was taking place. He described in valiant but not native English exactly how much

ice would have to form around the shell of hell before any
other American reporter or any reporter of any kind would
ever be invited to join the operation again.

As he railed on, I noticed a Norwegian flag tacked to the wall
behind him. *"Snakker De norsk?"* I asked ("Do you speak
Norwegian?").

He stopped, said nothing for a few seconds. Then, like a
Hollywood comic of the 1940s pulling an absurd reversal, he
said, "You've got big feet, but there's a pair of boots on the
other side of the bed that might fit you. Try 'em on!"

All night long we stood there waiting for the shadows to tell
us another group of refugees had arrived on the far bank of the
canal. Then we'd push the raft into the water and play out the
rope as our two boatmen paddled across. One would get out
and help four or five Hungarians into the raft. When the raft
was loaded, the boatman still in the raft would tug on the rope
and we'd pull it back over. Then the lone boatman would pad-
dle over again and repeat the process until all the refugees were
on the Austrian side. The second boatman came back with the
last load.

We had to wait at least an hour to an hour and a half between
refugee clusters. I was the coldest I've ever been in my life, and
there was no place to huddle behind or curl up inside. All we
could do was stand there and wait. Light wasn't the only thing
prohibited. So was talk. Normal speech travels surprisingly far
over frozen flatland, and it was important not to betray our
position to the Communist patrols. We were only allowed to
whisper softly to the person immediately ahead of us on the
rope and the person immediately behind.

I tried to remember what day it was. It was Thursday. It had
only been the previous Saturday night when I'd taken a
Norwegian girl, Meta Heiberg, from Woman's College to the
Carolina Theater in Greensboro, North Carolina, where we
saw newsreels of almost the very spot where I was now standing. When the screen showed Hungarian refugees pouring into
Austria, Meta had said, "My sister Karen's over there somewhere helping those people." That was all.

The next day I got the call inviting me to fly over with the air force. On Monday I flew. And here I was, freezing and waiting and marveling at the courage of the boatmen who voluntarily put themselves into jeopardy every time they crossed to the other side of the canal.

Eventually I decided to avail myself of whispering rights. The figure in front of me was so roundly bundled against the cold I couldn't tell if it was male or female. I leaned forward and said, "My name is Barry Farber and I'm from America."

A woman's voice replied, "My name is Karen Heiberg and I'm from Norway."

The cold, the power of the coincidence, and the tension of the border all combined to keep me from maximizing that opportunity. All I managed to do was flatfootedly utter the obvious: "I took your sister Meta to the Carolina Theater in Greensboro, North Carolina, five nights ago."

The effect on Karen was powerful. I can't complain, but I wish I'd been quick enough to add, "She sent me over here to find out why you never write Uncle Olaf!"

How I Married Hungarian

You don't launch into the study of a new language casually. But it's not quite as solemn a decision as an American man proposing to his girlfriend after an evening of wine and light jazz. It is, however, something like an Ottoman sultan deciding to take on another wife. It really is like a marriage. Something in you actually says, "I do!" and you decide to give it time and commitment that would ordinarily be invested elsewhere.

My pledge never to try to learn Hungarian was shattered by Hungarian heroism, Soviet tanks, and my agreeing to help Hungarian refugees resettle in Greensboro. I wasn't the only journalist who stayed on that story long after history moved on. Every journalist I know who got involved in any part of the Hungarian Revolution became attached to it.

I started in Munich in the transit refugee camp for those fleeing Hungarians who were destined to go to America. I buzzed from one refugee to another like a bee to blossoms, drawing as many words and phrases as I could from each and writing them down.

The U.S. Air Force gave its Luitpol barracks over to the Hungarians, who promptly plastered their own signs right on top of the English signs on all the doors. The door that once said "Doctor" suddenly said *"Orvos."* The door that once said "Clothing" suddenly said *"Ruha."* And so on. It was easy to tell who among the Americans and Germans at Luitpol were genuine language-lovers. They were the ones who were not annoyed.

The Hungarian relabeling of everything at Luitpol actually gave me my most explosive language-learning thrill. When I went searching for a men's room, I found myself for the first time in my life not knowing where to go. You don't need Charles Berlitz to take you by the hand to the right one when the doors read *"Mesdames"* and *"Messieurs," "Damen"* and *"Herren," "Señoras"* and *"Señores,"* or even the rural Norwegian *"Kvinnor"* and *"Menn."*

No such luck prevailed at Luitpol. The two doors were labeled *"Nők"* and *"Férfiak."* I looked at those two words, trying not to let my language-lover's enthusiasm distract from the pragmatic need to decipher which one was which relatively soon.

My thinking went like this. The *k* at the end of both words probably just made them plural. That left *Nő* and *Férfia,* or possibly *Férfi.* Something came to me. I remembered reading that Hungarian was not originally a European language. It had been in Asia. The Chinese word for "woman," "lady," or anything female was *nö*—not *no* and not *nu,* but that precise umlaut sound that two dots over anything foreign almost always represents. (I lose patience with language textbooks that spend a page and a half telling you to purse your lips as though you're going to say *oo* as in "rude" and then tell you instead to say *ee* as in "tree." If you simply say the *e* sound in "nervous" or "Gertrude," you'll be close enough.)

Following that hunch I entered the door marked *"Férfiak."* The joy that came next should arise in tabernacles, not men's rooms. To my satisfaction and relief I walked in and found five or six other *férfiak* inside!

Back in America I went looking for some books and records (there were no cassette tapes in those days) to help me in Hungarian. There were none. Communist rule had so completely cut Hungary off from the West that when you went looking for a Hungarian book, the shelves of even the biggest bookstores leapfrogged Hungarian, jumping right from Hebrew to Indonesian. There was one Hungarian-English phrase book published by a New York Hungarian delicatessen and general store named Paprikas Weiss. To accommodate the wave of Hungarian immigrants who had come to America in the 1930s, they had published their own little phrase book, which was distinguished by its utter failure to offer a single phrase of any practical use whatsoever to those of us working with the refugees. It was loaded with sentences like *Almomban egy betőrővel viaskodtom,"* which means, "In my dream I had a fight with a burglar"!

Finally, like supplies that lag far behind the need for them in wartime, some decent English-Hungarian/Hungarian-English dictionaries arrived—no grammar books yet, just dictionaries. An explorer named Vilhjalmur Stefansson went to Greenland one time and proved you could live for eighteen months on nothing but meat. I proved it was possible, with nothing but that dictionary, to resettle a half-dozen Hungarian refugees who spoke no English at all in Greensboro, North Carolina, to care for all their needs, and have a good deal of fun *without one single bit of grammar!*

Hungarian has one of the most complex grammars in the world, but grammar is like classical music and good table manners. It's perfectly possible to live without either if you're willing to shock strangers, scare children, and be viewed by the world as a rampaging boor. We had no choice. Hungarians had to be talked to about homes, jobs, training, money, driver's licenses, and the education of their children.

"Tomorrow we'll go to the butcher's," for instance, had to do without the thirty-nine grammatical inflections a Hungarian sentence of that length would properly entail. We did it with nothing but the translation of essential words: "Tomorrow go meat fellow." "A charitable woman is coming by to help you with your furniture needs" became "Nice lady come soon give tables chairs."

I learned Hungarian fluently—and badly. Many years later I decided to return to Hungarian and learn it properly and grammatically. It's a little like being back in Latin class, but this time I have a much better attitude.

New Friends

For the next thirty-five years I stood my ground and resisted taking up any new language. The languages I'd studied up to that point included Spanish, French, Italian, German, Portuguese, Dutch, Norwegian, Danish, Swedish, Russian, Serbo-Croatian, Chinese (Mandarin dialect), Indonesian, Hungarian, Finnish, Yiddish, and Hebrew. I happily applied myself to building competence in those languages and turning a deaf ear to all others.

It was tempting to tackle Greek; so many Greeks I could have practiced with were popping up in my daily travels, but I clung to my policy of "No more languages, thank you!" That policy was misguided; in fact, swine-headed. I was like the waiter standing there with arms folded who gets asked by a diner if he knows what time it is and brusquely replies, "Sorry. That's not my table!"

I could have easily and profitably picked up a few words and phrases every time I went to the Greek coffee shop and in the process learned another major language. But I didn't. In the 1980s immigrants to New York, where I lived, began to pour in from unaccustomed corners of the world, adding languages like Hindi, Urdu, Punjabi, Farsi, Bengali, Pashtu, Twi, Fanti, Wollof, Albanian, and Dagumbi to our already rich inventory of

Spanish, Chinese, Italian, Yiddish, Portuguese, Greek, Polish, and Hebrew. I abandoned the policy. Now I want to learn them all—not completely, just enough to delight the heart of an Indian or African cab driver who never before in his entire life met an American who tried to learn his language.

PART TWO

The System

Do as I Now Say,
Not as I Then Did

A wise man once said, "I wish I had all the time I'd ever wasted, so I could waste it all over again." Others may look at me and see someone who can, indeed, carry on a creditable conversation in about eighteen languages. I'm the only one who knows how much of my language-learning time has been wasted, how little I've got to show for all those years of study, considering the huge hunks of time I've put into it. In fact, I feel like one of those hardened convicts who's occasionally let out of jail under armed guard to lecture the sophomore class on the importance of going straight.

If I had it to do all over again, I wouldn't do it at all the way I did then. I'd do it the way I'm doing it now, the way I will detail in this book. It's the way I've finally grown into and the way I hope you will proceed in order to get the absolute most out of your language-learning dollar and your language-learning minute.

Here are some of the myths I held dear in the years when I thought I knew how to study languages, myths I now want to trample before you get the slightest bit seduced by them.

I'll put on my language cassettes while I work around the house and learn the language as easily as I learn lyrics to popular songs.

Great image. It just doesn't work. You can't just push a button and let the language you want to learn roll over you. Expecting to learn a language by laid-back listening is like expecting to build a magnificent body by going to the gym, sitting in the steam room, chugging a glass of carrot juice, and then bragging about your "workout"!

You're going to have to study the material on that cassette, capture every word, learn it, review it, master it, and then *check-challenge* yourself after every piece of English. (We'll consider a "piece" to be whatever the speaker on the cassette says in English before you hear the target language. It may be a word, a phrase, a whole sentence.)

Abandon all images of language learning that resemble lying on a tropical beach and letting the warm surf splash over you. Pretend instead, as you listen to your cassette, that you're a contestant on a TV game show. After each piece of English, ask yourself, "For one thousand dollars now, quick, how do I say that in the language I'm trying to learn?"

Since I'm not in school anymore, time isn't important. I'll take my time, skip a day, skip two days; the language will still be there when I get back to it.

Spoken like a true linguaphony. A language has a lot in common with a military foe. Don't let it rest. Don't let it regroup and devise fresh ways to foil your attack. Keep up the rhythm of your offensive. Keep your momentum going. (This is only an illustration of tactics, of course; no language is an enemy.) A program that features disciplined effort will convince you that you're serious and generate fresh inspiration and energy.

This chapter I'm studying now is hard and probably not too important. I'll skip it and get back to it later on.

That's a giant-killer. The declension of the numbers in Russian. The subjunctive in the Romance languages. The double infinitive in German. The enclitics in Serbo-Croatian. The noun cases in Finnish. Almost every language has formidable mountains to climb. Don't walk around them. Climb them! Take one step at a time. Just be careful never to surrender to the temptation to beg off the hard stuff and learn only those parts of the language you find congenial.

It will seem masochistic, but I want you to learn the names of the letters of the alphabet in your target language and the grammatical terms too, so that when you ask a native how a certain word is spelled, you can bandy the letters back and forth *in the language.* When you ask a native for the past tense of this verb or the negative plural of that noun, do your asking in the target language.

I'm never going to pose as a native speaker of their language, and I'd never be able to pull it off even if I tried, so why bother to develop the right accent?

Nobody is arrested for indecent exposure just because he dresses poorly. On the other hand, a person unconcerned about dress will never impress us with his appearance. It's the same with the proper accent. As long as you're going to go to the trouble of learning a language, why not try—at very little extra cost—to mimic the genuine accent.

A poor accent will still get you what you want. A good accent will get you much more.

If you can put on a foreign accent to tell ethnic jokes, you can put one on when you speak another language. If you think you can't, try! A lot of Americans believe they're unable to capture a foreign accent when subconsciously they're merely reluctant to try. We're all taught that it's rude to make fun of foreigners. That childhood etiquette is hereby countermanded. "Make fun" of the foreigner's accent as effectively as you can as you learn his language.

Your "infancy" in a foreign language is spent learning to grope with incomplete phrases made up of incorrect words to mash your meaning across. "Babyhood" comes when some of the phrases are complete and more of the words are correct. "Childhood" arrives when you can deal rather fluently with concepts involving bread, bed, buttons, and buses, even though you can't yet discuss glassblowing in Renaissance Estonia.

"Adulthood" is being able to discuss absolutely anything, but with a pronounced American accent. With "maturity" you acquire a creditable accent in the language. You'll know you've achieved maturity when you become annoyed at other Americans you hear plodding through the language with no effort to "foreignize" their accent to approximate the correct one.

Be content with partial victories. I rejoiced the moment I learned I could speak Swedish well enough to convince a Norwegian I was a Finn. I celebrated when I realized I could speak Serbo-Croatian well enough to convince an Italian I was a Czech!

There will come a moment when I will cross a border and earn the right to say, "Yes, I speak your language"!

There's no such border. Learning a language is a process of encroachment into the unknown. When can you say you "speak a language"? The famous ophthalmologist Dr. Peter Halberg of New York refuses to consider that he speaks a language unless and until he can conduct a medical lecture in the language and then take hostile questioning from his peers. By his standards, he speaks only five languages!

My standards are less exacting. I'll confess to "speaking a language" if, after engaging in deep conversation a charming woman from a country whose language I'm studying, I have difficulty the next morning recalling which language it was we were speaking.

The Language Club, about which I will say more later, has a valuable guideline. When anybody asks a Language Clubber, "How many languages do you speak?" he gives the only safe answer, "One. I speak my native language." He lets a breath go by to let that "one" sink in, after which he may then add, "However, I am a student of . . ." and mentions as many languages as he likes.

To the question, "Do you speak such and such a language?" the all-class response is a James Bond smile and three words: "Yes, a little." It's much better to let people gradually realize that your "little" is really quite a bit than to have them realize that your "Yes, I speak such and such" is a fraud.

Say you've been studying Indonesian, far from a commonplace language, and to your amazement (and delight) one of the other guests for dinner is from Indonesia. Repress the instinct to yelp at your good fortune. Act at first as though you know nothing of Indonesian. Don't even say "Pleased to meet you" in Indonesian. There will be time. At the right point, much later in the proceedings, you'll have the opening to remark, "That's what the merchants of Djakarta would call . . ." and then let go your best burst of wit—in Indonesian.

For you actually to speak Indonesian and allow so much time to elapse before claiming your applause is downright noble. Beware flying socks when you lean over to your new Indonesian friend and, lowering your voice so as not to appear to be calling attention to yourself, finally unleash your evening's first volley of Indonesian.

Psych Up

Americans have grown up believing learning languages is hard. It is not hard! It merely seems hard because language instruction in American schools and colleges has until lately been so exasperatingly dull and unrewarding.

Grammar, I again protest, is usually presented in American classrooms as a kind of obstacle course designed to leave you gasping facedown on the Astroturf somewhere between the pluperfect and the subjunctive. Grammar can do that to you if you insist of attacking it the old way: frontally, rule by rule, exception by exception, with no fun en route and never feeling the joy of progress.

You're going to learn grammar, all right, but the conquest will never give you pain. You will waft through the thickest walls of grammar like a cartoon ghost and continue your journey onward through the language. Every time you look backward that wall will be lower, thinner, full of increasingly wider openings, and eventually it will disappear entirely. Contrary to centuries of American superstition, you don't have to conquer the grammar to possess the language. Conquer the language and you'll possess the grammar!

I've long entertained the fantasy of putting the old orthodox grammarians on trial for war crimes, the specific charge being assassination of the fun that flows from gaining command of another language. Their defense will predictably be "Bah, humbug. You can't immerse, converse, rehearse, or even play around with a foreign language without a good foundation in the grammar!"

They're right in insisting on the importance of grammar, but who says you've got to have it first, as some kind of brutal initiation? Where is it written that you must wrap cold, wet blankets of grammar around your eagerness to learn another language until it disappears? (Your eagerness, that is. The grammar never does.)

A six-year-old in America doesn't know what the word *grammar* means, but he knows to say "he does" and not "he do." How does he know? "He do" just doesn't sound right.

That's all! And that's enough!

Years later he will be taught that the English verb in the third-person singular of the present tense adds an *s* or *es* to the infinitive form, which serves uninflected for all other persons singular and plural.

You don't have to *know* grammar to *obey* grammar. If you obey grammar from the outset, when you turn around later and learn why you should say things the way you're already saying them, each grammatical rule will then become not an instrument of abstract torture disconnected from anything you've experienced but rather an old friend who now wants you to have his home address and private phone number.

When the grammatical rule comes first, followed by its pitiful two or three examples in the textbook, it seems to the student like an artificially confected bit of perversity rolled down upon his head like a boulder.

When the grammatical rule comes after you've got some of the language in you, it becomes a gift flashlight that makes you smile and say, "Now I understood why they say it that way!"

So, you are right now and forevermore warned not to bridle or to question, "Why is the word for 'go' in this French sentence *vais* and in the very next sentence *aller*?" Simply embrace

the faith that both sentences are correct and learn them like
Catholic children in strict parochial schools learn the Baltimore
Catechism.

The more shaken you become by grammatical storms, the
more tightly you must hug the faith. I vow it will all become
clear. And in this world. You won't have to wait for any other.

It's easy to reason, "Who am I trying to kid? They'll always
know I'm a foreigner. They'll excuse my mistakes. So forget
about all those rules. I just want to get by. Gimme some words
and phrases and get out of my way. As long as they understand!"

That's an attitude to be resisted. When you learn another
language, you will be accepted as an honored volunteer into
the culture of another people. Do you want to be accorded a
low rank or a high rank? Learn the language properly, which
means (eventual) conquest of the grammar. Don't be a buck
private when, for a few extra minutes of concentration, you can
be a general.

Look at it this way. Grammar is not a marathon run in which,
if you tire, falter, or fall, you fail. Grammar is an edifice you
must build on your property. But it doesn't have to be done all
at once. At the appointed moment in your studies, I will advise
you to master the first five lessons in your grammar book.
(Some call it a textbook or a workbook—it's the book they'll
give you at the bookstore if you ask, "Have you got anything
that teaches you French?") After that, you will advance through
reading, conversation, comprehension, and real-world contact
with the languages in addition to the grammar.

As I grappled with the complexities of grammar in Russian,
Finnish, Hungarian, and, to a lesser extent, German, I had
visions of those people way back when they were wandering
tribes. I imagined the tribal elders squatting around campfires
consulting with soothsayers who warned them, "In the mid-
twentieth century a child will be born to the Farber family in a
place they'll call America. He will try to learn our language. At
present it's too simple. Get back to work and come up with

some more grammar. Let our noun endings mire him up to his hips. Let the flesh of his face feel the thorns of our verbs. Flay his back with exceptions to our rules and let his hair get caught in our inflecting negatives and perfective aspects.

"Hurry!" the soothsayer concludes. "We haven't got a century to waste. Get in there right now and mess our language up so that poor guy will never get it!"

Now let the adult mind enter and make peace. Obviously, no language *tries* to be hard just to keep you out. Whatever rules you find perplexing in your target language, that language came by them naturally and organically. Grammar does change, but so slowly you'll never have to worry about it. Approach the grammar with a smile and your hand extended. That which you understand, take and keep. That which is confusing, return to again and again. That which seems impossible, return to again and again and again, until it becomes merely confusing. It will ultimately become clear. Meanwhile, however, you will be speeding ahead in your command of the language as you keep returning to those stubborn fortresses of grammatical resistance.

I can honestly say I came to like the study of grammar. Once you finally approach grammar with the right attitude, it becomes both a map that shows you the pathways through a language and a rocket that takes you there faster.

A paleontologist can find lifetime fascination with a fossil a child might ignore, kick, or toss into the lake just to hear the splash. Likewise, the grammar of various languages throws off some laughs and insights nonlinguists never get a chance to marvel at.

In German, for example, a woman doesn't achieve feminine gender until she gets married. The word for "girl" (*Mädchen*) and "miss" (*Fräulein*) are both neuter gender. In Russian, the past tense of verbs acts like an adjective; it doesn't shift forms according to person and number as verbs normally do, but shifts according to gender and number as adjectives do. In

Norwegian, Danish, and Swedish the definite article ("the") follows the noun and is attached to it. Therefore, "a field" in Norwegian is *en mark*. "The field," however, is *marken*. Romanian and Albanian, completely unrelated to the Scandinavian languages, do the same thing.

In Finnish, the word for "not" is a verb. (At least it behaves like a verb.) Finnish, alone in all the world, has an inflecting negative. In every other language in which verbs conjugate, the form of the verb changes according to person and number, whether the verb is positive or negative. Thus, in Spanish the verb meaning "to want" goes *yo quiero, tu quieres, el quiere*. If you wish to say "I don't want," you keep the verb forms the same and throw the word for "not," *no,* in front of it (*yo no quiero, tu no quieres, el no quiere*).

In Finnish, and this is pure believe-it-or-not to anyone who's looked at a lot of different languages, it's the word for *not* that does the changing! Thus, "I want," "you want," "he wants" in Finnish goes, (*minä*) *haluan,* (*sinä*) *haluat,* (*hän*) *halua.* In the negative, however, the verb for "want" becomes *halua* in all persons and the word for "not" changes from person to person. Thus, "I don't want," "you don't want," "he doesn't want" becomes (*minä*) *en haluaa,* (*sinä*) *et halua,* (*hän*) *ei halua.*

I think my most impossible-to-top discovery is the fact that in Hindi and Urdu "tomorrow" and "yesterday" are translated by the same word. Once, a Pakistani cab driver actually seemed irked that I found that to be at all strange. "We have verb tenses to tell us which is which" was his testy explanation.

American feminists have mounted crusades to convert sexist terms that have over the years insinuated themselves deep into the language. We've all abandoned *chairman,* for example, for the cumbersome but less provocative *chairperson, manhole* for *maintenance hole,* and so on.

It's strange that the most blazing example of language sexism has gone unreformed, even though it occurs in some countries with active and successful feminist movements. Maybe it's because, unlike *manhole, this* sexism is more than just a word or a term. It's gone through the bone into the marrow, through the words of the language into the grammar.

You may remember it from Spanish 1. You may have gotten it right on the tests and not thought of it since. I refer to the Romance language "gender-surrender" from feminine to masculine.

Let's say two women are having lunch. If you want to refer to them in Spanish, the word is *ellas,* the feminine "they" or "them." If they should be joined by a man, however, the *ellas* becomes *ellos,* masculine for "they" or "them." And no matter how many more women show up and crowd around the table, the Spanish language can never put that humpty-dumpty *ellas* back into play—unless the lone man leaves!

Theoretically, a million women can be rallying in the main square of the capital. The newspapers will report that *ellas* rallied, made demands, did thus and so. If, however, one man wanders into the square to join in, the proper pronoun is *ellos!* And that same rule goes for French, Italian, Portuguese, Romanian, and a few other languages.

You may never come to love grammar, but work with it. Although sometimes annoying and in thick disguise, it's your friend.

French or Tagalog:
Choosing a Language

What are your language objectives?

This is not merely one of those abstract questions universities and fitness centers like to annoy you with before they accept your application.

Are you planning to marry a German and live in Germany? Then the language you want to learn is German. You should stick to German and learn it well. Do you own a hardware store in a neighborhood of a growing American city where your customers represent eighteen different language groups, including Tagalog and Punjabi? Then you want to learn greetings, key business expressions like "invoice" and "charge account," and the names of as many items in your inventory as you can in eighteen different languages, including Tagalog and Punjabi.

The way you're going to spend your language-learning hours depends on your objectives.

We're going to presume here that whatever language you choose to learn, you want to learn well. If you merely want to learn a smattering of greetings and phrases in a lot of languages, great. You're in for a lot of fun, particularly when you see, if you haven't already, how far even a few words can carry you. In that case, the departure from the method outlined here is obvious. You don't need mastery of the grammar. Most big bookstores offer racks of phrase books for travelers in up to twenty-five different languages. Buy all you want and study your favorite ten or fifteen of the first hundred phrases in each.

Don't feel frivolous if you feel you want to learn a language but don't know which one. You're part of a movement to correct a weakness that has bedeviled America since the founding of our nation. Do you like opera? Try Italian. Diamonds? Try Dutch. Commercial advantage? German or Japanese. Cutting-edge positioning for the world down the road? Chinese or Arabic. East-West barrier-breaking and door-opening? Russian.

French is second only to English as an international language, spoken far beyond the borders of France itself. Spanish enables Americans to become more complete citizens of the Western Hemisphere, while a resurgent Spain itself becomes an increasingly important part of Europe.

If willingness of subject peoples to learn the language of the conqueror is any indication of the conqueror's popularity, then the winning conqueror is England and the loser is Russia. Those forced into Moscow's postwar empire had an aversion to learning Russian, but in spite of Communism's failure, the Russian language remains the most widely spoken of the Slavic languages. It can be your key to the dozen or so related languages (Polish, Czech, etc.).

Maybe you want to learn a difficult language, like Finnish; an easy language, like Indonesian; a useful language, like French; or an obscure language, like Albanian.

My motives for learning various languages have ranged from chance and youthful energy (Norwegian) to wanting a vital tool for my work (Spanish) to processing refugees (Hungarian) to getting dates with women whose looks I liked (Swedish) to proving I wasn't an idiot for almost flunking Latin (Chinese).

Nobody who sells language-learning books and devices will ever frown in disappointment at your choice of a language.

Don't feel you have to apologize or explain that you want to learn Czech—or Catalan or Yoruba or Urdu or Kurdish—for no other reason then you're tired of walking around a world as exciting as this one speaking only one language!

Gathering Your Tools

You've decided which language you're going to learn, and you've made a deal with the grammar of that language: you agree to learn it, and in return it agrees not to rush you, bore you, discourage you, or hurt you.

Now it's time to go shopping. Find a bookstore that offers a broad selection of language-learning materials. Don't settle for one where the clerk is not sure but says, "We might have something in French and Spanish over in 'Language.'"

BASIC TEXTBOOK

Find a basic book (textbook, workbook) that gives you a good grounding in the grammar of the language. Never mind if it seems to give you grammar and little else. Never mind if it reminds you of the books that depressed you back in high school and college. We'll find all the excitement—reading and conversation—elsewhere. Grammar is all you need from this one.

DICTIONARY

Most language dictionaries are two-way: English-French (or whatever) and French-English. Make sure the dictionary you buy at least lives up to that. (I have walked out of bookstores with dictionaries I assumed were two-way that turned out to be only one-way, and the way I wasn't looking for!)

A lot of dictionaries are infuriatingly inadequate. They don't even have words like *negotiate* or *proprietor*. Spend a little time making sure you're getting something substantial. It's a good idea to look through a newspaper and make a list of some of the more complicated words in the news columns. Those are the words you'll soon be looking up. Does that dictionary have them? Price, color, and the neatness with which the dictionary fits into your pocket, briefcase, or handbag are a lot less important than finding a dictionary that can deliver.

PHRASE BOOK

Buy a phrase book for travelers. Berlitz publishes a series in eighteen languages, and others keep popping up in bookstores and the racks of airport newsstands. They're inexpensive and easy to use. These books, smaller than a piece of toast, offer little or no grammar, but they bristle with practical words and phrases, listing the English followed by the foreign language and then a transliteration that guides the rankest beginner to an understandable, usually a creditable, pronunciation.

Don't be put off by the naïveté, inexpensiveness, superficiality, and comparative weightlessness of these travelers' phrase books when laid alongside your impressive dictionary and your complex grammar book. Good zoos need hummingbirds as well as elephants.

NEWSPAPER OR MAGAZINE

Find a newspaper or magazine in your target language. Most big cities have newsstands where you can buy publications in a dazzling variety of different languages. Otherwise, call the nearest consulate or embassy of the country whose language you're out to learn. Usually they're proud and pleased to help you. If you have a choice, go for a publication from that country itself, rather than one published by immigrants from that country in America. Certainly no foreign-language publication printed in America is likely to contain language *more* authentic than publications printed in the home country, and it may very well be less authentic.

A friend of mine who set out to learn French immediately bought a subscription to *Le Monde*, a popular Paris daily. That's overkill. If he were to learn every word in any one issue of *Le Monde*, it would be "mission accomplished." One issue of one publication in your target language at this point is all you need.

STUDENT READER

It may be difficult, but if possible see if you can locate a schoolbook or some reading material from the country at about a sixth-grade level. Such books are obviously excellent bridges from the rudiments to the real world. If you can't find one, never mind. Your newspaper or magazine will seem elementary to you soon enough.

PORTABLE TAPE PLAYER

The invention of the handy portable cassette tape player catapults language-learners from the ox cart to the supersonic jet. You can now inhale a foreign language through your ears. "You can't expect me to do two things at once!" is a bygone complaint. Listening to foreign-language cassettes as you go about your daily deeds is a high form of doing two things at once.

The Walkman (or any such tapeplayer) is an electronic can opener for whatever language you're learning. Formerly we had to chew through the tin.

CASSETTE COURSES

There are many cassette courses in many foreign languages. They range from "travel" cassettes, really simple tourist phrase books set to sound and costing between ten and twenty dollars, clear up to multicassette study courses that carry the student into advanced levels and cost between one and two hundred dollars, or more.

Don't dismiss the least expensive ones as "superficial little travel cassettes." If you master every word, every phrase, every pronunciation, and every grammatical point contained in even the simplest of those cassettes, you can consider yourself advanced.

There are basically four kinds of cassettes for the study of foreign languages. We'll call them *flat single-rep, flat double-rep, formatted,* and *cultural.*

The *flat single-rep* cassettes, usually the least expensive, give you the English word or phrase followed by the foreign equivalent uttered only one time.

The *flat double-rep* cassettes are the same, except the foreign phrase is repeated twice. (When you begin making your own study cassettes, you'll repeat the foreign piece three times.)

The *formatted* cassette puts theories of instruction into practice and follows systems that some highly successful language teachers have found effective. For example the Pimsleur method, named after the late Dr. Paul Pimsleur, takes the student by the ear and guides him through the language as though it were a Disneyland exhibit. Unfortunately Dr. Pimsleur died before he could personally develop courses in a large variety of languages to advanced levels. His techniques, however, are being applied to more courses in more languages by Dr. Charles A. S. Heinle of the Cassette Learning Center in Concord, Massachusetts.

The Pimsleur method provides the best minute-by-minute "learning through listening," thanks to several strokes of Dr. Pimsleur's innovative genius.

First of all, you become a participant. Pimsleur doesn't let you merely listen in hopes your lazy mind will help itself to some of the new words being offered on the smorgasbord. After five minutes with any Pimsleur course you will always harbor a certain disdain for all cassette courses that merely give you a voice saying something in English followed by the equivalent in the target language. Pimsleur pricks your wandering mind to attention by asking, for example, "Do you remember the Greek word for 'wine'?"

Theoretically, that little trick shouldn't make a spectacular difference. After all, you bought the course. You want to learn the language. Why should the teacher on cassette have to find ways constantly to recover your attention? The unfortunate truth is that the average mind plays hooky whenever possible. The difference between Pimsleur asking, "Do you remember the Greek word for 'wine'?" and a voice simply saying "wine" is, as Mark Twain once put it, "the difference between lightning and the lightning bug!"

Nor does Pimsleur always settle for the simple verbal prompt. A typical Pimsleur tactic is to demand, "You accidentally bump into a man getting on the bus. What do you say?" That ingrains the foreign phrases for "excuse me" far more than a rote recitation of the words themselves.

Pimsleur's "graduated interval recall" achieves what I call the "pinball effect." When the steel ball in the pinball machine nears the bottom, you can manipulate the flippers to catch the ball and send it all the way back to the top again. Likewise, at the very instant when your mind is about to let a new word or phrase "fall to the bottom," Pimsleur zings it in again, sending it back to the top of your awareness. This time it doesn't sink so fast. When it does, Pimsleur hits it again.

Pimsleur gives you a pause on the cassette after each question he asks you. In the early going there's a temptation to stop the machine while you flounder for the answer. Don't! Learn to try to come up with the answer during the pause provided. That will more than teach you the word. It will train you to have that word ready for action at all times. It's marvelous to feel your growth as you relisten to your Pimsleur lessons, succeeding more and more each time at delivering the required word before the teacher's voice rolls over you with the next question.

Berlitz is the most famous name in language instruction, and except for the Berlitz Travel Cassettes, which are flat single-rep, all their cassette courses are formatted. The Berlitz Basic Courses, available in French, Spanish, German, and Italian, feature ingenious conversations between teacher and students, and their top-of-the-line Berlitz Comprehensive Courses are really dazzling soap-opera-like sagas filled with romance, treachery, suspense, and drama. Both the basic and the comprehensive courses sneak massive payloads of grammar and vocabulary into the student's repertoire.

Cultural cassettes aren't really language-learning cassettes at all, but many people suppose they are and buy and sell them as such. Songs, plays, readings, stories, and poems in foreign languages are indeed helpful, but shouldn't be mistaken for the "high-protein" intake needed to build command of a foreign language. They're great relaxers, tests of how far you've come, adjunctive exercises, and ways of letting the foreigner know that you view his language as more than just a briar patch of irregular verbs.

The cultural cassettes are the condiments. The others are the entrées.

AUDIO-FORUM

No wine-lover's heart ever leapt higher in France, no rug-lover's heart ever leapt higher in the Teheran bazaar, no diamond-lover's heart ever leapt higher in downtown Antwerp than the language-learner's heart will leap at the sight of Audio-Forum's catalogue.

Their credulity-defying inventory of language courses keeps growing, so it's hard to say exactly what they have at any given moment. But on May 1, 1998, for example, Audio-Forum's catalogue offered 279 different courses in 97 different languages!

To Audio-Forum there's no such thing as Arabic. They offer moderately priced courses in Eastern Arabic, Egyptian Arabic, Levantine Arabic, Moroccan Arabic, Syrian Arabic, Lebanese Arabic, and more.

Their French selections consume seven full catalogue pages and include Basic French, Business French, French videos, Conventional Cajun French, Regional Accents of France, Mystery Thrillers in French, French Radio Commercials, French Folk Songs, French Scrabble, and a course in French street slang for less than $20.

You can get courses in Literary German, Cultural Italian, Executive Japanese, Ballet Russian, Medical Spanish, Religious Portuguese, Cinema Hungarian, Survival Tibetan, Computer learing programs in many languages, twelve Native American language courses, and much, much more.

There's a nominal charge for their catalogue. Audio-Forum's address is 96 Broad Street, Guilford, Connecticut 06437. Their toll-free number is 1-800-243-1234.

BLANK CASSETTES

We have do-it-yourself gasoline pumps. We do not have do-it-yourself eye surgery. It may seem strange to some (and wildly objectionable to others) to recommend do-it-yourself language cassettes starring *you* in the language *you* are trying to learn. Orthodox language teachers are likely to consider that something akin to doing your own eye surgery.

I've found it extremely helpful. At some point you will have gotten the hang of pronunciation sufficiently to push the record button of your cassette player and recite your own words and phrases onto a blank cassette. Your pronunciation will not be good. It may be bad. But the value of being able to listen to a cassette with the words you need and want at the moment— rather than a cassette prepared by somebody with no knowl-

edge of you, your desires, or your needs—much more than outweighs the disadvantage of your imperfections.

So, get blank cassettes—the shortest possible—so you can
start building a cassette library of the words and phrases you
want to know to supplement those the educators who produced
all the standard cassettes decided to teach you first.

It's better to know the word—its meaning, its spelling, its use
in sentences—even if you have to listen to it in your unskilled
accent, than not to know the word at all.

FLASH CARDS

Printed flash cards are available in the major languages.
They're about the size of business cards and usually provide a
vocabulary of a thousand words. Flash cards are the most
underrated language-learning tool of all. They've been around
for decades and go widely unused, even by those who own
them.

Flash cards commonly list the English word (plus related
words) on one side of the card and their foreign equivalents on
the other. Some sets of flash cards give you a little grammar at
no extra cost, adding to the word itself the forms of that word
a student of the language should know.

The language student should reach for a fresh stack of flash
cards before he leaves home in the morning as instinctively as
a policeman reaches for his badge. The flash cards, more than
any other tool, can help the student take advantage of the day's
"hidden moments," the secret weapon upon which the promise
and the premise of this method is based.

Learn how to keep your flash cards handy. Whip them out
and flash-test yourself the instant you find yourself with the
time. (The person you're walking with stops to look at a shop
window. You've read the menu, finished the newspaper, and
the waiter hasn't come yet. The clerk has to validate your credit card. There's a line at the bank or the ticket counter. The elevator seems to be stopping on all floors.) Learn how to draw

those cards out and start flashing even if all you'll have is five seconds. If the person you're telephoning doesn't answer until the fifth ring, he's given you time to go through two or three entries. Learn to be quick. I've learned how to master a whole new Chinese character between the time I dial the last digit and the time my party says hello.

BLANK FLASH CARDS

Whether you can locate prepared flash cards in your target language or not, go to your nearest stationery store and get a hefty supply of blanks. As you travel through the language you'll constantly come across new words, modern slang, special phrases you'd like to know, cute sayings a native speaker teaches you at a party, and the like. Capture them immediately on your blank flash cards and carry a stack with you at all times. In later chapters when we learn how all these tools interrelate, you'll realize the importance of your own homemade flash cards. Purists may quarrel about recording your own foreign-language vocabulary-building cassettes. Nobody can quarrel with you preparing your own flash cards.

STURDIKLEERS

Sturdikleers are the handy celluloid or plastic packets that protect passports, driver's licenses, etc. Find the size that best accommodates a stack of flash cards and pick up as many as you need, or more.

FELT HIGHLIGHTER PEN

You'll need a felt pen to mark all the words in your newspaper or magazine that you don't know. Choose a color that highlights but doesn't obscure the word when you mark it.

Those are your tools. Now let's go do the job!

The Multiple-Track Attack

So is there really a magic way to make learning a foreign language painless?

Yes and no. We have some magic, all right, tricks and tactics that literally shovel the language into your head, as opposed to your high-school Spanish class that teaspooned it in or didn't bother getting it in at all. The system, however, won't work unless *you* do. There's going to be pain, but you will have something—plenty—to show for it.

The promise here is not gain without pain. It's the *most* gain for the *least* pain.

If you suddenly decide to get physically fit (just as you've decided to learn another language) you wouldn't sit around and wonder, "Let's see. We've got aerobic exercises, free weights, stretching, high-tech gym machines, jogging, swimming, vitamins, and sensible nutrition. Which one shall I use?"

Obviously, you're going to use a mix of some or all of the above. And that's the way to approach learning another language. The multiple-track attack simply parts from the absurd notion that you should choose a grammar book *or* a cassette course *or* a reader *or* a phrase book; instead, it sets you up with *all* of the above—and more—simultaneously.

You will fail or you will succeed. If you fail, your books, cassettes, dictionaries, and scattered flash cards will litter your drawers and closets like so many unlifted barbells, unswallowed vitamins, unsoiled workout suits, and unused jogging shoes. They will mock you every time your embarrassed eye falls upon them.

Succeed, and you'll be the proud owner of another language.

Charles Berlitz says that saying a word or phrase aloud ten to twenty times is more effective a learning technique than merely reading the same item fifty to one hundred times. Likewise, seeing a word or phrase in your grammar book fifty times does not secure it in your memory as effectively as seeing it two or three times and then coming across that same word or phrase by surprise in a newspaper or magazine or hearing it on a cassette or in a radio broadcast or a movie or in conversation with a native speaker.

It may be hard to explain why the multiple-track attack works, but it's easy to prove that it does. It's somehow related to the excitement of running into someone from your hometown on the other side of the world. You might have ignored him back home or dismissed him with a "howdy," but you'll be flung into each other's arms by the power of meeting unexpectedly far from home.

The rub-off effect kicks in nicely almost from the beginning of your effort as words you learned from a flash card or cassette pop up in your workbook or newspaper. Sure, you will eventually conquer the word even if it occurs only in your grammar book or your phrase book or on your cassette, but that learning involves repeated frontal assault on a highly resistant unknown. Let that same word come at you, however, in a real-life newspaper article and your mind embraces it as an old friend.

Attempting to master a language with a grammar book alone is too boring; with phrase books alone, too superficial; with cassettes alone, too fruitless (except with Pimsleur!); and with dictionary and newspaper alone, impossible. The multiple-track attack makes your work pay off.

Getting Started

Open your grammar to the first lesson. Do you understand the first paragraph? If so, proceed to paragraph two. If not, reread paragraph one. Can you determine precisely what it is that's blocking you from comprehension? If so, take a pencil (not pen) and underline the word or words that are tripping you up. Run a wavy pencil line down the left-hand margin of whatever confuses you. That paragraph will never change. The grammatical point that the confusing paragraph seeks to make will remain as immutable as Gilbraltar until your mind decides to open up to it. Comprehension frequently clicks on like a light switch. No rush.

Try to summarize whatever you don't understand. Pretend you're writing a letter to your aunt complaining about this ridiculous new language you're trying to learn and, using as few words as possible, encapsulate your confusion in writing. Take that note and put it in a Sturdikleer holder and carry it with you in your pocket or bag. Get into the habit of writing down everything that confuses you and carrying it with you. You will try to find informants or mentors—either native speakers or others who've learned your target language well enough to answer your questions. Befriend the Korean grocer, the Italian waiter, the Albanian at the pizzeria, your dentist's Romanian secretary. You don't need such people, but they're extremely helpful and easier to locate than you might think, and getting easier all the time as America becomes an international mixture of peoples. Your informants will usually love being asked to help you learn their language.

Let's suppose you've stubbed your venturesome toe on paragraph one or two or three or whichever, and no comprehension clicks on. At this point you must consciously overturn the rules of misdirected American language teaching and do something radical. You must wave good-bye to your unsolved puzzle and keep moving ahead.

If you don't understand it, skip it for the time being. Chances are excellent your confusion will clear itself up as you progress through more and more concepts you *do* understand. You will have the pleasure of looking back on earlier lessons in the grammar, seeing your wavy pencil lines beside a now-clear paragraph, and saying to yourself, "How could I have ever been derailed by *this*?" It's fun erasing those wavy lines!

Continue through five lessons of the grammar before you so much as glance at any of your other tools. Leave the cassettes wrapped in their packaging. Don't be tempted to look at the newspaper or magazine in your target language. The more of a language-lover you are, the tougher it will be. Plodding through grammar while friendly cassettes and real-life newspapers await will make you feel like a child who has to finish his homework before he runs out and plays baseball. And that's exactly the point. You *are* a child in that new language, and like all children, you have to learn to put first things first. Grammar comes first. Build a little character by slogging through five chapters of it. You will build up a head of steam that will send you charging headlong into more pleasant terrain.

Cassettes, newspapers, flash cards, and phrase books will cut the boredom out of waiting for buses and replace it with growth in another language; these will be your reward after you make an honest beginning in the grammar. Sustain your spirit during the grammar study by reminding yourself how soon you're going to be allowed to go out and "play."

Into the Real World

When you've served out your sentence of five lessons of grammar, spread out all your other tools (you should regard them as "toys") and prepare to use them all simultaneously.

Take the newspaper or magazine. Go to the upper left-hand

corner of page one. (In languages like Arabic and Hebrew, that will be the upper right-hand corner of the "back" page, which is their front.) That article is your assignment. It will easily be the toughest newspaper article you've ever read. And it will just as certainly do you more good than any other.

Take your highlighter and highlight all the words you don't know in the first paragraph. You may very well end up with a colored line through every single word in that paragraph. After all, this is no schoolhouse text that dips to your beginner's level. This is as real-life and real-world as an exercise can get. And all you've had so far is five lessons of elementary grammar. Never mind. Play the game and dutifully mark through every word you don't know, even if it be every last word in that first paragraph!

Then reach for your dictionary and your blank flash cards. Go to the first word and look it up. One of four things will happen: (1) You'll find the word exactly as it appears in the newspaper. (2) You'll find a word that starts out the same but seems to go haywire halfway through or at the end. (3) The word will not be in your dictionary (even though you gave that dictionary a "sophistication" test before you bought it). (4) You will think that word is not in the dictionary because the word has done crazy things with itself. It's altogether possible, owing to rules of that language you haven't learned yet, that the role of the word as it appears in the newspaper demands it be written differently from the base form, which is the one listed in the dictionary. (The word *vaya* in Spanish, for example, won't be in the dictionary. It's the singular imperative form of the verb *ir* meaning "to go.")

In case 1, the word is in the dictionary spelled exactly the way it is in your newspaper (from now on we'll say "text"—it could be a magazine or even a book). Take a blank flash card and write the English on one side; then flip it over and write the foreign word on the other. Write in block letters so your flash cards will always be easy to read. I hesitate to labor the procedure for making your own flash cards. There is a pre-ferred procedure, however, and I herewith present it in case you don't already know it.

Single words and entire phrases are best handled differently. When you write individual words on your flash card, you need only a "short runway," so treat the card in its "tall" (vertical) form rather than its "fat" (horizontal) form and enter your words one under the other down the length of the card. Write the English word across the "forehead" of the card, then flip it, not sideways, but head-over-heels, and write the foreign word across the opposite forehead.

Then turn the card back over to the English side and write your next word directly underneath, turn it over and write in the foreign word, and keep repeating until the card is filled. That head-over-heels lengthwise flip makes the card easier to manipulate in a crowded bus or elevator and less likely to fall out of your hand.

When you graduate to writing entire phrases on your blank flash cards, it's obviously better to treat the card in its fat form. Continue to flip head-over-heels.

Now, case 2: You find a word in the dictionary that seems as though it's trying to be the word in your text but it falls off track: the ending changes spelling. You've probably found your base word, all right, but the word in the text, for reasons you don't yet comprehend, has taken another form. Is it a verb? Then the dictionary will give you the infinitive form (*to be, to do,* etc.), whereas the form in your text could be one of many variations, depending on person, number, tense, or, in some languages, aspect.

If that riff of grammatical terms makes you feel like I felt on my fifth day of Latin class, fear not. Language teachers would prefer to assume that such grammatical jargon is familiar to every graduate of an American high-school English class. Alas, that assumption is grossly misguided. But help is here. The "Back to Basics" chapter later in this book will explain all nec-

essary grammatical terms in friendly, nonthreatening language
that requires no prior understanding of grammar.

Write the base form—the dictionary form, that is—on your
flash card and try to decipher the meaning of the text with that
base form as clue.

If the meaning is clear, don't worry yet about why the word
in the text differs from the base form. Part of the fun of this
process is having that knowledge surrender itself to you as you
proceed through your grammar book. If the meaning is not
clear, make a "question card," spelling the confusing word the
way it appears in the text. Keep your Sturdikleer with question
cards with you at all times. When you meet your informant, or
anybody who can explain your confusion away, pull out the
question card and your miasma of confusion will become
windshield-wiper clear.

List no more than six unknown words per flash card. Don't
clutter the card. It's a good idea to draw a line under both the
English and the foreign word, giving each entry its own "cubi-
cle" on the card. Also, check carefully to make sure you don't
omit either the English or the foreign word, giving you a situa-
tion in which English word number three on the card fails to
correspond to foreign word number three. (I once went around
for almost a year thinking the Russian word for "prince" meant
"raspberry jam"!)

In cases 3 and 4, either the word's not in the dictionary or it's
not there in any form that's recognizable to you. Enter the
word on a question card.

You may have four or five complete cards, eighteen or twenty words defined and ready to be learned, from the first paragraph in your text alone. Put those cards in clear plastic and
carry them with you at all times. Don't mix them up with the
question cards. Keep them separate. The cards with the dictionary forms of the foreign words from the text you didn't know,
with their English equivalents on the reverse side, are the
beginning of your collection of linguistic growth protein.

Advance!

Now you're ready for paragraph two. Between paragraphs one and two, you've been glancing at those flash cards during your hidden moments—waiting in line, on elevators, etc. With highlighter poised like a sword, you now sally forth into the second paragraph.

The going will probably be noticeably easier, because paragraph two will likely be dealing with much the same subject matter as paragraph one and many of the words will be repeats. Step back and note how many fewer colored lines marking unknown words there are in paragraph two. Never mind that those are repeat words. If you knew them from flashing your cards in the interval between tackling paragraph one and tackling paragraph two, then it's clean conquest. Bask in it, and move on to paragraph three.

No cheating! Don't let your possible lack of interest in the subject matter of the text tempt you into junking it and jumping across the page to another article that looks like it's about something that interests you more. No soldier fighting in the arctic would dare ask his commanding officer if he might be excused to go fight in the tropics. Advance! Charge! Slog through it one step—one word—at a time.

By the time you reach the end of page one, if it's a newspaper, you will note with glee that the colored markings indicating words you didn't know, almost solid in the early paragraphs, will have diminished precipitously by the end of the page. That page is a progress chart.

And you'll have what seems like a ton of flash cards loaded with words in varying degrees of surrender to you. Carry as many flash cards with you as possible, and rotate them regularly so your attention is evenly parceled out among them.

Tradition-bound teachers would have problems with that kind of "ice plunge," a naked leap into a foreign-language newspaper after only five lessons of grammar with nothing for help but a dictionary, which in many cases can't help because you won't know the various disguises (changing forms) of many of the words. What's the point?

There are several. America is a nation of people who make straight A's in intermediate French and then get to Paris and realize they don't speak intermediate French! The knowledge that the text—newspaper, book, magazine, whatever—is a real-world document that does not condescend to a student's level is a tremendous confidence-builder and energizer for your assault upon your target language. The awareness that you're making progress, albeit slowly, through typical text, genuine text, the kind the natives buy off their newsstands and read in their coffee shops, gives even the rank beginner something of the pride of a battle-toughened marine.

Memorize Your Part

You are now, let's say, beginning chapter six of your grammar book and fighting your way valiantly down the first column of your text. Keep going on both those fronts, and pick up another tool.

Open your phrase book and read the introduction carefully, paying particularly close attention to the rules of *transliteration*. All such books will have three columns: the English word or phrase, the foreign-language translation, and then the transliteration, which is your guide to proper pronunciation using the English alphabet.

When you get the hang of the language, you won't need the transliteration crutch. Until you do, you need it totally. But note that there is no recognized standard system of transliteration. The International Phonetic Alphabet is supposed to be, but nobody uses it because learning it is almost as hard as learning another language itself.

There are at least half a dozen ways to transliterate the capital of China. The Chinese Communists prefer *Beijing*. The

Chinese Nationalists prefer *Peking*. If that were the only word you wanted to learn and there were no need for you to learn transliteration systems, we could write it *Bay-jing*, adding that the *Bay* is pronounced like the English word for the body of water and the *jing* like the first syllable of "jingle."

Your phrase book will take mercifully little space to tell you how to pronounce the words according to their chosen system of transliteration. Usually in less than a page you'll be told to pronounce *ai* like the *y* in "sky"; *ei* like the *eigh* in "weigh" and so on through all the needed sounds. Some phrase books indicate which syllable gets the stress by placing an accent mark on top of it, others by capitalizing every letter in the syllable. Don't be impatient because you suddenly feel you're called upon to learn another written language which is neither English nor the language you're trying to learn. Look upon the transliteration guide as your opportunity to learn the combination to a safe that will let you help yourself to the correct pronunciation of every word in that book!

Advance now to the first page of phrases in the phrase book. Your newspaper didn't teach you how to say "How are you?" and it's a good bet the first five lessons of your grammar didn't either. Here it comes! This is your first chance to learn how actually to say things.

"Yes." "No." "Please." "Thank you." "You're welcome." "Good morning." "Good afternoon." "Good evening." "I'm very pleased to meet you." "How are you?" "Very well, thanks; and you?" "Fine."

You'll master these precious nuggets of real-life communication quickly. But don't stop with merely mastering them. Use that phrase book and plot a conversational pattern, a routine you go into when you meet someone who speaks your target language. Treat it as though you're memorizing your part in a play.

"How do you do?" "My name is _____." "What's your name?" "Where are you from?" "How long have you been here?" "I don't speak your language well." "How do you say

that in your language?" "May I get you something to drink?" "I
don't understand." "Would you please repeat?"

Here again, traditionalists would frown. "That's not learning
a language," they'd protest. "That's just learning how to parrot
a few phrases!"

And right they'd be, if that were all you were doing. But you
are now accumulating flash cards with vocabulary and moving
through lesson seven or eight of the grammar, so don't feel you
have to apologize for learning how to parrot a few handy
phrases.

Your ability to bandy some useful phrases is a motivator.
There you are, *speaking the language!* Isn't that what you started
all this for? Admittedly you're not debating the economic con-
sequences of his government's latest reversal on tariff agree-
ments, but you are asking someone if he's too cold and telling
him you hope to meet him again.

More magic happens when you're at that peak motivation.
You find yourself acquiring more material, more conversational gems gleaned from his end of the conversation. Remember,
you're a confessed beginner. When you don't understand
something, you're excused for asking him to repeat it, spell it,
write it down on one of your blank flash cards. (Always carry
some.)

It's gratifying, in fact, enthralling, to enter your next conversation with your powers to converse enhanced by the previous
encounter.

A note of caution, however. Eventually you may find yourself able to small-talk so fluently you'll mistake that ability for
having arrived. Back to the newspaper and the grammar with
you before such thoughts corrupt!

Add Cassettes

For most of the history of the world, there was no way the self-
taught language student could hear the language spoken. He

had to rely on printed rules, grossly inadequate, to guide him in pronunciation of his target language.

Then came the phonograph record, which seemed like ideal deliverance from darkness, until the tape recorder came along, followed quickly by the portable cassette tape recorder, which allowed language-learners to pick up earphones and listen to a wide variety of foreign-language fare as they jogged, shopped, ran errands, or walked to work.

As is the case with many technological breakthroughs, disappointment followed. The closets of many fine, otherwise strong-willed people are littered with the wreckage of once beautifully packaged foreign-language cassette courses. They thought technology had replaced study. They thought all you had to do was pop a cassette into the machine, press a button, and take in the language like a car takes in gasoline.

Remove that inflated expectation, resolve to do your part, and the invention of the portable cassette tape player will indeed fulfill its promise to the language-lover endeavoring to become a language-learner.

Are you presently armed with the right cassette course?

Unless your cassette was mislabeled and carries lessons in a language other than the one you'd like to learn, it's a good learning aid. It may not be the best. It may be far behind the best, but so what? It will offer you words and phrases in your target language with native accuracy in pronunciation.

You no more want to limit your hearing of the language to one cassette course than you'd want to confine your tennis playing to one partner. The ideal cassette library is one in which the student can pull down a cassette for review in rotation and not quite remember how the dialogue goes or what's coming next. A little mystery, rather than rote familiarity, aids the student ear in its difficult mission of paying attention.

Within certain obvious limits, you can buy literally every course in your target language that's commercially available and still describe your adventure with the language as "inexpensive."

In your beginning stages you should insist on cassettes that come with a written transcript of everything recorded. (The Pimsleur courses are an exception. Their integration of written-word exercises and their back-and-forth interaction between teacher and student more than excuse the absence of word for word transcription.)

It's a good idea to follow the text visually as you listen to the cassette the first few times. As you get a little bit familiar with the target material, divorce the two. Take the cassette and the tape player with you. Listen even when you can't follow the written text. Read the text even when you can't listen. You'll find the two excellent reinforcers for each other.

If your cassette course is flat single-rep or flat double-rep, keep listening over and over and try to capture as many words and phrases as you can.

When you're ready—actually, long before you're ready— challenge the cassette to a duel. Start at the beginning and see how many words and phrases you know. After the English, stop the cassette recorder with the pause button and ask yourself, "Do I know it in the target language? Do I almost know it? Do I know any part of it—how the word or phrase begins, how it ends, what major sound characterizes it? Do I know enough to give myself credit for at least partial conquest?"

Don't be in a rush to release the pause button and see how well you did. Make a teasing game of it. Make yourself wait for the fulfillment of hearing the term in the target language. That will make a stronger hit into your memory. Drop a weighty object from a higher tower than previously and it will sink deeper into the mud.

Then move on to the next term. It's a little like playing soli-taire; no matter how you write your own rules, it still retains the arresting power of a game. Maybe you'll ask yourself if you can score one out of five correct; later, one out of four. It's hard to imagine it in the early going, but you will eventually play the game by seeing if you can get every term on the cassette correct from beginning to end. But that's not quite total victory. Total victory is seeing if you can do it without stopping to think.

And then, if your machine has the mechanism, try it at accelerated speed!

Hidden Moments

They taught us the fable of the tortoise and the hare so early, most of us dismissed it as a children's tale and ignored the powerful lesson it contains: Others may be brighter. Others may learn quicker and retain more. Yet whosoever keeps on plodding relentlessly toward the goal of mastering another language, though his gifts be dim, stands a better chance than the unmotivated genius whose dazzle ignited so much envy in high-school Spanish class.

Harnessing your hidden moments, those otherwise meaningless scraps of time you'd never normally think of putting to any practical use, and using them for language study—even if it's no more than fifteen, ten, or five seconds at a time—can turn you into a triumphant tortoise.

By now you're slogging your way through the grammar and enjoying it more (or suffering it less) than you did in college because you no longer feel obliged to dwell upon a knotty point until you understand it before moving forward. You will not fail a test or risk a bad grade if you abandon some grammatical black hole that tries to swallow you, and move on ahead.

You're battling your way through the foreign-language newspaper, your slow progress mitigated by the awareness that this is the real world and the daily language won't get any tougher than that text.

You're cherry-picking through your phrase book, learning how to say practical things in your target language and rehearsing all those precious phrases as though they were your part in a play.

Your cassettes are beginning to bore you without teaching you a great deal (yet).

You're amassing a flash card collection.

By now you've probably met someone from the country whose language you're learning and, like a rookie cop about to make his first collar, you risked your ego by attempting a greeting. He laughed appreciatively—and answered you in English.

Hidden moments will heal your deficiencies soon enough, but first let's talk about the *un*hidden moments, the study time you've arranged to commit to your endeavor. This book is written for those who can't or don't want to expend the time or money required to take formal classes. Successful self-teaching is our objective. If you can take a whole hour every day and devote it to your studies, you're in an excellent position to make satisfying, even dramatic, progress. If you can devote a half hour a day, you're still poised for success.

If you can't commit a regular block of time, if the best you can do is an hour here, a half hour there, and maybe a three-hour block of time over the weekend, that's satisfactory, provided you keep it up and maintain momentum. Gardens unattained go to weed. Apples bitten into and abandoned turn brown. Likewise, your collection of language data—words, phrases, rules, and idioms—will dissolve into a useless mass if not kept up.

Apportion as much time as you reasonably can and as regularly as you can, and then enjoy the magic as the hidden moments kick in.

A professional financial advisor on radio once urged people to take careful inventory of their financial assets, promising that overlooked and forgotten riches were to be revealed at every hand. Her credibility disappeared for me at that moment. I honestly think I've never been at a point in my economic life where I was likely to underestimate my holdings by as much as seventy-five cents!

When it comes to *time,* however, that's a much more lucrative matter!

You can learn a language in twelve months using only those moments you didn't realize you had.

We've already mentioned a few corners in which hidden moments lurk awaiting liberation. Let's review them and add some more.

Moments we instinctively bid good-byes to include those spent waiting for and riding in elevators, waiting for the person you're dialing to answer, waiting while he puts you on hold, waiting for a long outgoing message from someone's answering machine to reach its conclusion. There are those moments when you're helplessly trapped—when someone who's too good a friend to hang up on delivers an unending narrative requiring no verbal participation on your part beyond an occasional grunt, groan, "dear me," "gee whiz," or other appropriate interjection to let him know you're still there. It's usually safe to divert some of your attention from your friend to your flash cards.

That's a major payload of hidden moments right there, and we haven't even gone beyond the elevator and the telephone! We can take time back from our days just like the Dutch took land back from the sea and put it to work.

What do you normally do when you're waiting in line at the bank, the post office, the airline counter, the bus or train station, or the supermarket checkout counter?

What do you do while you brush your teeth? You could be listening to a language cassette. What plans have you made for the time you're going to spend waiting behind your steering wheel at the gas pump? Or waiting for the rinse cycle? Waiting for the school bus?

You get the point. An honest, thorough scrutiny of your normal week will yield dozens, even hundreds, of minutes that can be put to work learning your target language. And don't forget, a scrap of time need be no longer than five seconds to advance you closer to your goal.

Arrange your life so you will never be caught without something to study in your target language. If you carry a briefcase or a pocketbook, your grammar book or newspaper, even your dictionary, can be your companion. Phrase books are usually so thin they easily fit into a coat pocket. There's nothing holy about your foreign-language newspaper. Cut off a page and fold it up and carry it with you, along with your highlighter.

Certainly we can all agree there's no excuse ever to get caught without flash cards. The instant you get stymied—on line at the cash machine, waiting for a store clerk, etc.—pull out your deck of flash cards and get to work.

If your hidden moment only lasts five seconds, giving you time for only one flash card, give that flash card five seconds of the right kind of effort. Look at the English. Suppose it says "shoe." Say to yourself something like, "What a great moment in my life. I presently do not know the word for 'shoe' in my target language. Within seconds that infirmity will be erased! I will get a look at that word and, though it may not lodge in my memory after one single flash, that word will eventually be mine." Make a big deal of it. Indeed, it *is* a big deal when you expand your vocabulary. Now flip the card. If your target language is Spanish, the other side of the card will reveal the word for shoe as *zapato*. Once we hand you the ultimate vocabulary memory weapon, the one developed by Harry Lorayne, you will put that word through a mental process that will make it easier to retrieve. Right now, just try to remember it any way you can, even by rote.

Proceed to the next card, or the next word on that card. You should have enough cards with you so the same word doesn't pop up so quickly that you haven't really tested your retention, but not so many cards that you don't meet the same word for another two or three days.

The fun comes when you meet the word again. Imagine that word is your opponent in a duel. Is it going to be you or he?

Look only at the English. Try to remember. Don't flip the card until you're certain you're defeated and cannot possibly come up with the word.

Even grizzled multilingual veterans who've used this system successfully will find themselves letting their guard down and moving from the English word on the flash card to the foreign word too quickly. No challenge, no effort, no gain.

There's no memory glue better than standing there, in the line at a bank or whatever, looking at the English side of a flash card, not knowing the word immediately, trying hard to bring it back, fearing you can't, and refusing to give up. Suddenly you think you have it. You flip the card over and see that you were, indeed, correct!

That word has no more chance of escaping you than your middle name.

Eye-Ear and Ear-Only Moments

So far your hidden moments have been those that could be utilized either for reading (flash cards) or listening (cassettes). Let's call them *eye-ear* moments. When you're walking through town or through the park, jogging, riding in a bus or train too crowded for reading, or driving or riding in a car at night, obviously you can't play with flash cards. These are, however, also hidden moments that offer exquisite opportunities for foreign-language infusion.

Let's called them *ear-only* moments.

A good rule is to use eye-ear moments for eye functions (flash cards, grammar book, newspaper), leaving ear functions (cassette listening) for those moments when you couldn't be reading anyhow. More simply, when you can listen *or* read, read. Save your listening for when you can *only* listen.

Cassettes En Route

When I dramatize this system of language-learning at seminars for the Learning Annex in New York and other educational organizations, displeasure clouds the brows of the students when I urge them to "wrap the university around their heads" (put on their earphones) and study their cassettes as they walk, run, amble, or do errands around the neighborhood. There's an attitude of "Enough, already. I've done my language workout for the day. Let me enjoy my walk or my run and take in nature and the landscape."

This claim may sound inflated until you test it, but leisurely strolls and nature walks, far from being dampened, are actually enhanced by cassette listening en route. You can invent little listening games that make it fun. I, for instance, may start the cassette and listen until I reach the first word in the target language I don't already know. I'll then stop the cassette player and concentrate on capturing that word for the remainder of that city block. When I reach the curb of the next block, I'll start the tape until I reach another word I don't know and repeat the process.

There's a happy kind of synergy when you realize you're exercising *and* you're learning; you're enjoying the beauty of the surroundings *and* you're growing. You can slow down. You can settle for "collecting a few new words" as you might collect a few blossoms or a few seashells. You can turn off the tape for a while and throw the earphones back over your neck and inhale and enjoy. Don't separate your life into "fun" and "study." Harmonize language study with your activities.

Get your cassettes into action when you wake up, stretch, make the bed, fix breakfast, brush teeth, dry off after bath or shower, wash dishes, and so on through all the moments when those less ambitious turn on the radio or TV. Don't forget, passive listening is better than nothing, but not by much! Engage the English mentally and try to beat the voice on the cassette to the foreign word.

"Harnessing hidden moments" is a three-word course in language learning all by itself. It offers a side benefit that has nothing to do with learning languages but has a lot to do with enjoying life.

Look at those other people, those unfortunates who, unlike you, have no intention of harnessing their hidden moments to learn languages or anything else. Look how they wait like zombies in line, their faces masks of boredom and pain. *Your* boredom and pain will vanish the instant you get into line and whip out your flash cards.

Learning languages can become incidental to daily life. It's often fulfilling enough just having something useful to do! Remember what Dean Martin said to the slowly sipping starlet: "I spill more than you drink!" Just by using the minutes you'd otherwise spill, you can learn another language.

Harry Lorayne's Magic Memory Aid

How does a farmhand feel the day the tractor arrives, after he's plowed by hand for thirty-one years? Undoubtedly the way I felt when, after decades of memorizing foreign vocabulary the old way, I suddenly discovered Harry Lorayne and his methods.

Harry Lorayne became well known some years ago as the world's leading "memory magician." His feats of memory for names and faces, complex numbers, and hundreds of objects he could repeat forward, backward, or in scrambled order enlivened many a late-night TV show.

Harry Lorayne was to be a guest on my WOR radio show one night to talk about his book on improving memory. It was his seventeenth or eighteenth book on memory and, as I was looking it over, I saw a short, almost hidden chapter entitled "Memorizing Foreign Language Vocabulary."

I sped to that chapter and my language-learning life changed completely from that moment forward. I think I actually cried in rage at all the time I'd wasted attempting rote memory of foreign words during the thirty-one years I had studied languages before I met Harry Lorayne!

Let me invite you now to pay one last visit to the old way of learning foreign-language vocabulary before we wave it an untearful good-bye. Imagine facing a page containing a hundred words in a foreign language. You only know eight or nine of them, you have a test tomorrow morning at eight o'clock, and your roommate is playing the radio too loud.

You sit there with your palms pressed over your ears repeating those unrelenting syllables over and over, hoping enough of them will stick by dawn to give you a passing grade.

Did you enjoy that kind of learning? Are you nostalgic for it? If so, enjoy the recollection now. After the following pages you will never tackle new vocabulary that way again.

In the fourth or fifth grade, when Miss Hobbs was teaching us the rudiments of music, my class accomplished an amazing feat of memory in one flash (many of you probably had the same experience). The notes on the five-line music staff, E, G, B, D, and F, could easily be remembered with the help of the simple phrase, "*E*very *G*ood *B*oy *D*oes *F*ine." What's more, we learned that the notes in the spaces between the lines were F, A, C, and E, or, as even we ten-year-olds guessed, the word "face." Who could ask for anything more?

Harry Lorayne teaches us we can ask for everything more! He teaches a system of association—called *mnemonics*—that allows you almost always to bring forth any word in conversation whenever you want it.

The way to capture and retain a new word in a foreign language is to sling a vivid association around the word that makes it impossible to forget. Lasso the unfamiliar with a lariat woven from the familiar.

We'll now take a random assortment of words in various languages and demonstrate how it works.

The Spanish word for "old" is *viejo*, pronounced *vee-A-ho* the middle syllable rhyming with "hay." Imagine a Veterans Administration hospital—a VA hospital—that's so old and decrepit they have to tear it down and build a new one. Before they lay in the dynamite the crew foreman calls the contractor and tells him, "We don't have to waste dynamite on this VA hospital. It's so *old* I can knock it over with a *hoe!*"

Got it? A *VA* hospital so *old* you can knock it over with a *hoe*. Therefore, "old" equals *V-A-hoe*, and that gives us *viejo*. (*Viejo* is stressed on the next-to-last syllable: *vi-E-jo*; in our code, *v-A-hoe*.)

Readers of much skepticism and little faith will worry that spinning such an involved yarn to capture one word is less productive than spending the same amount of time simply repeating the word to yourself over and over again. Wrong. The yarn, like a dream, takes much longer to tell or read than it does to imagine. And you'll quickly see for yourself how helpful the yarn is when it comes time to retrieve the word and use it.

As you continue now through further demonstrations of this technique, try to challenge the examples. See if you can think of better ones. A "better" one is simply one that works better for you.

We're going to swing headlong now into dozens of sample "lassos," associations designed to rope your target word and bring it obediently to your feet, never again to part. Ignore the fact that many of the examples that follow teach words in languages you're *not* trying to learn. Never mind, I tell you, never mind! Learn the system and you will use it happily and effectively ever after in the language of your choice.

The French word for "anger" is *colére*, pronounced *cole-AIR*.

Strange, we associate anger with heat. We say "in the heat of anger," but when someone is angry at us, we say he's "cold," "chilly," "giving us the cold shoulder." It's not too much of a leap to imagine an angry person radiating his anger, spilling it off in all directions, in the form of cold air. You hope he's not angry, but when you enter his office, you know your hopes were in vain because you can feel the *colére*, the "col' air" (*cole'-AIR*).

The Russian word for "house" is *dom*, pronounced *dome*. Imagine your amazement upon landing in Moscow and seeing all the houses with *dome*-type roofs. Or imagine marveling at how "*dom*estic" the Russian men are.

The Italian word for "chicken" is *pollo*, pronounced exactly like the English "polo" (*PO-lo*). Imagine your Italian host urging you to join him for an unbelievable spectacle. An Italian impresario with a gift for animal training has staged the world's first polo match between teams of chickens! You're thrilled that you're going to be able to go back to Gaffney, South Carolina, and tell your friends you saw *chickens* playing *polo*!

The Italian word for "wife" is *moglie*, pronounced *MOLE-yay*. Imagine you're a man about to get married and you get a friendly tip from an indiscreet clergyman that your bride-to-be is known to have a strange animal as a pet and fully intends to bring that animal into your home after the nuptials.

You're torn! It's too late to call off the marriage. All the relatives have been invited and the paperwork is all in. Besides, you love her. You decide to barrel forward and hope for the best.

As the organ plays and the preacher intones the vows, all you can think of is, "What kind of animal is it? Is it a lion? Is it a tiger? Is it a slick and sneaky snake? A giraffe?"

When the two of you arrive at your threshold after the honeymoon, the suspense ends. She brings forth a pleasant little cage containing a cute little furry creature.

"This is my pet mole," she says. "He's going to live with us."

You cry forth your relief. "Hooray!" you shout. "It's only a *mole*. It's only a *mole*!" you cheer, "*Yay!*"

It's only a *mole-yay*. Your wife's secret animal is nothing more than a *mole*, therefore, "*Yay!*" "Wife" equals *MOLE-yay*.

WAIT A MINUTE!

An enemy, a skeptic, even a queasy ally at this point could say, "Wait a minute. I'm trying to learn a language. I'm not sure I want to walk around with a headful of images of wives who keep moles, chickens that play polo, angry people emitting cold air, and VA hospitals you can knock over with a hoe!"

You won't! One beauty of the system is, the association that helps you capture the word falls away and disintegrates. Once you've learned the words, the "crutch" obligingly disappears.

A common form of the verb "to speak" in Hebrew is *med-aber*, pronounced *meda-BEAR*. There it is: you were walking through the newly planted forests of Israel and suddenly you *"med"* a bear who could *speak!*

In Indonesian, "movie screen" is *lajar*, pronounced almost exactly like "liar" (*LI-ar*). Easy. The man is rapidly winning the woman's heart in the movie, but you don't wish him well because he's such a *lajar!*

"Horse" in Russian, transliterated into English script, is *lo-shad*, pronounced almost exactly like *LAW-shod*. You try to bring your own horse with you into the Soviet Union, but at the border the Soviet customs officer tells you Sorry, he'd like to accommodate you, but your horse doesn't have horseshoes and, according to Soviet *law*, all horses must be *shod*.

"Horse" equals *LAW-shod*.

The Greek word for "grape" in English transliteration is *stafilya*, pronounced *sta-FEEL-ya*.

You're in a Greek vineyard in the mountains near Albania. You see the most luscious grape you've ever laid eyes on. As you reach for it, the air is split with a squeaky voice screaming, "Don't touch me!"

"I'm sorry," you sputter, retreating in shock and shame. "I wasn't going to eat you. It was *just to FEEL you* (jus' *sta-FEEL-ya*)."

"Grape" equals *sta-FEEL-ya*.

The Serbo-Croatian word for "lunch" is *ručak*, pronounced almost exactly like *RUE-chuck*. You're having lunch in a restaurant in Yugoslavia. The waiter overhears you making a political remark he doesn't appreciate, so he throws you out bodily. Never one to go quietly, you pick yourself up out of the gutter, dust yourself off, and, just before you head for the American Embassy to protest, you shake your fist at the waiter through the window and vow he'll *rue* the day he *chucked* you out while you were having *lunch*.

"Lunch" equals *RUE-chuck*.

"Plate" in Indonesian is *piring*, pronounced exactly like the English "peering" (*PEER-ing*).

Your Indonesian restaurant experience is a bit more pleasant than the one in Yugoslavia. You walk in and find yourself suddenly becalmed by the serenity of the dining room. All the Indonesians seem to have their heads bowed in prayer. You ask the headwaiter if you've interrupted some sort of religious service.

"Not at all," he assures you. "They're not praying. We just got our new *plates* with mirrored surfaces and they're all *peering* at themselves to see how they look!"

"Plate" equals *PEER-ing*.

The Farsi word for "cheaper" transliterated into English is *arzontar*, pronounced *our-zone-TAR*.

The hotel in Teheran is filled, but the clerk tells you it's a warm night and he'd be happy to rent you sleeping space on the roof. You're delighted to learn you're paying only half what the other roof-sleepers are paying, until you get to your designated spot on the roof, at which point you exclaim to your spouse, "Now I see why our spot is *cheaper*. All the other tourists are sleeping on those nice ceramic tiles. *Our zone,* the spot assigned to us, however, is *tar!*"

"Cheaper" equals *our-zone-TAR*.

"Potato" in German is *kartoffel*, pronounced exactly like *cart-AW-ful*.

You buy potatoes from a *cart* and they turn out to be *awful.* "Potato" equals *cart-AW-ful.*

Stop right here! Do you remember the Spanish word for "old"? Or the French word for "anger," the Italian word for "wife," the Serbo-Croatian word for "lunch," or the Indonesian word for "movie screen"?

When we display this system of word-capturing at seminars for the Learning Annex, there's a collective gasp when, after spelling out an association to capture the tenth word, we suddenly stop and ask how many can recall word number one, four, and so on. At no point did we suggest that the students try to recall the words used as examples as we laid out the system. When they see that almost everybody recalls every single one of them anyhow, the students realize this system contrasts well with the kind of rote learning they'd tried earlier. One grateful participant exclaimed, "This system teaches you words you're not even *trying* to learn. The old way doesn't teach you no matter how hard you try!"

The Almosters

The skeptic has one shot left before he's wiped out by the power of the method. He can, at this point, say, "Hold it! Every word you've used to demonstrate the system so far falls much too neatly into our lap—*liar, mole-yay.* It's a setup. It's not real. Very few words will cooperate with the system once you tackle the real world!"

And he's right! The words we've been subjecting to the memory system so far are *automatics.* They fall right into your lap with self-suggesting images. Only a small percentage of words will fall into the system as facilely as the automatics. More, many more than you imagine, will fit automatically into the system, but far from enough to conquer another language. Never mind! Behind the words that fit neatly into the system are many times that number of words that, while fitting nowhere nearly as neatly, can nonetheless take you so close to the target word that true memory can easily complete the job. We call those words *almosters*. Of our four groups — *automatics, almosters, toughies,* and *impossibles* — the almosters make up by far the biggest single category.

Let's demonstrate.

The Chinese word for "lobster" is transliterated as *loong-shah,* pronounced very much like *LOAN-shark*. If you imagine that lobster is so expensive you need a *loan shark* to negotiate a *lobster* lunch, true memory will easily putt you from *loan-shark* to *low-shah*.

Shrimp in Indonesian is *gambiri,* pronounced *gam* to rhyme with "Tom" followed by "beery" (*gam-BI-ri*). You complain to your waiter in Indonesia that the chewing gum he served you tastes awfully beery. He advises you it's not chewing gum, it's shrimp. Your putt will take you from *GUM-beery* to *GAM-beery*.

The Serbo-Croatian word for "spoon" is *kasika,* pronounced *KASH* (to rhyme with "gosh")-*ee-kah*.

You want to get a spoon in Belgrade. They send you outside the hotel to a *cash-and-carry* to get a *spoon* if you want one.

Or if you're familiar with the Eastern European grain called kasha (buckwheat groats), you can imagine dipping your *spoon* into a bowl of *kasha* in the back seat of your *car*. True memory will carry you from *kasha-car* to *KASH-ee-ka*.

"Spoon," then equals *KASH-ee-ka*.

The Italian word for "day" is *giorno,* pronounced *JUR* (as in "jury")-*no*. You're eagerly awaiting the outcome of a legal action, but the *jury* has been tied up all *day* with *no* verdict. Even stronger would be the notion of eagerly awaiting the outcome of the trial and learning that the whole day went by without the jury even showing up! All *day* and *jury no*.

"Day" equals *JUR-no*.

"Humid" in Persian is *martoob,* pronounced *mar* (as in "marshal")-*TOOB* (as in "tube"). It's so dry in central Iran that in order to provide comfortable *humidity* in your room, the *mar-*

itime authorities arranged to bring water in through a *tube*.

True memory will easily let you lop off all but the first syllable of "maritime" and change the vowel sound from the *a* as in "maritime" to *a* as in "marshal" so that "humidity" equals *mar-TOOB*.

"Banana" in Indonesian is *pisang*, pronounced PEA-*song*, the second syllable rhyming with the *cong* in "conga." You'd long heard of jungle magic in the outer islands of Indonesia, but you never really believed in it until you went to the local grocer looking for bananas. You don't see bananas anywhere. You ask if he has any bananas. Sure, he says, plenty. "Excuse me," you say, "I don't see any." Be patient, he begs you, until he finishes with a customer.

When it's your turn he asks you how many bananas you want. You reply, half a dozen. He then takes six *peas* and sings them a mysterious little *song*. Before your bewildered eyes, they turn into *bananas!* The *peas* that were *sung* to became *bananas*.

Your only putt is to make the final vowel sound like the *o* in "conga."

So "banana" equals PEA-*song*.

The Spanish word for "to iron" is *planchar,* pronounced *plan* (to rhyme with "Don")-CHAR (as in "charcoal"). The hotel in Madrid has an excellent reputation, with only a single and rather bizarre lapse. Apparently a maid with too much seniority to be fired has a habit of leaving the iron on the backside of the trousers so long it leaves burn marks the size of the iron itself smack across both buttocks.

You have no choice. Your paints need ironing and you've got to take your chances. To improve your odds you gingerly approach the concierge and say, "Excuse me, sir. Could you please find out if the maid plans to *iron* these pants correctly or if she *plans* to *char* them? Your putt is to carry the *plan* sound from one rhyming with "tan" over to one rhyming with "Don."

"To iron" equals *plan-CHAR*.

The Indonesian word for "donkey" is *keledai,* pronounced almost exactly like "call it a day" without the *it.* That's what donkeys in hot climates are reputed to want to do after carrying their loads, and that's what we'll now do with this particular series of examples.

Un-American Sounds

So far we've shied away from words containing sounds that don't exist in English. The real world won't be so protective.

"Un-American" sounds are exaggerated as an obstacle to progress in most languages. I say that not because it's unimportant to master the sounds correctly, but because most of them will enter your repertoire automatically with practice. The trilled *r* in Spanish, the French *r* that sounds as though it issues from inside the pituitary gland, the half-*sh* half-guttural in German, the double consonant in Finnish, the many umlauted *u*'s and *a*'s and *o*'s in the various European languages will all be explained in your grammars, and better than explained on your cassettes: they'll be *pronounced.*

Many languages carry so many markings and so many different *kinds* of markings over and under certain of their letters you may be intimidated. Almost all of them are empty threats; despite their sinister-looking foreignness, they don't convey any sounds we don't have in English.

The two dots over certain *a*'s in Swedish simply tell you that particular letter is pronounced as the first *a* in "accurate." Without the dots, it's the *a* in "father." There's no need to run from the Norwegian *o* with a line slicing diagonally down through it: the first *e* sound in "Gertrude" is close enough. Languages with the double consonant spend far too much time warning us Americans that this is something strange to us. It is not strange. We have double consonants too, maybe not inside the same word, but definitely inside the same phrase.

We pronounce the last sound of the first word and the first sound of the last word in "late train." We don't say "lay train." So much for the frightening double consonant.

We'll make no attempt here to teach the "click" sounds of some of the languages in South Africa or the larynx-twisting sounds of the Georgian language spoken in Soviet Georgia that actually sounds like paper ripping inside the speaker's throat. Those sounds are unrepeatable for most Americans and the languages in which they appear are mercifully obscure.

There is really only one sound that doesn't exist in English that we're obliged to learn well, and that's the guttural common in Hebrew, Arabic, Russian, Dutch, and several other languages.

Most textbooks are notoriously weak in conveying that sound. They know they're committing consumer fraud when, as they frequently do, they merely advise the American student to "approximate the *ch* sound in the German name 'Bach' or the final sound in the Scottish word "Loch.' "

However, "Bach" is *not* pronounced *bak*. "Loch" is *not* pronounced *lock*. "Chanukah" is *not* pronounced *Ha-na-ka*. The trick is to learn how to make the real sound.

The best method, though perhaps inelegant, is to imagine you're about to say the plain old *h* sound, and suddenly you feel a terrible tickle in the middle of your throat. The original *h* sound then becomes lost in all the other powerful things you now do. Clear your throat violently to eject the irritant causing that tickle. You will then have the "*Ch*anukah" sound, the "Ba*ch*" sound, the "lo*ch*" sound, the "*ch*utzpah" sound.

That sound has no natural parents in the English language. It's up for adoption. Stop and think what image comes easily to your mind that can make you hear that sound. Don't be afraid at first to exaggerate it. Then tone it down. Dry it out. It will soon be as serviceable and comfortable as the sounds you grew up with.

Gender

The Harry Lorayne method of remembering the gender of nouns in foreign languages makes you feel downright foolish for not having thought of it yourself!

In some languages you have to remember the gender of nouns in order to adjust the articles or the endings of the adjectives that go with them. All the Romance languages— Spanish, French, Italian, Portuguese, Romanian, etc.—have masculine and feminine gender. Usually, but far from always, you can figure which is which by the word's ending: *o* for masculine, *a* for feminine. French, however, conceals gender clues with noun endings as unrevealing as battlefield camouflage. German and Russian have masculine, feminine, and neuter nouns. The Scandinavian languages call their two noun genders "common" and "neuter," as does Dutch. Chinese, Japanese, Indonesian, Hungarian, and Finnish, like English, have no noun genders.

How now do we remember whether the French noun for "train," also spelled *train,* is *le train* (masculine) or *la train* (feminine)? It happens to be masculine, *le train.* Imagine not merely a train that has no women passengers, but a train that doesn't allow women passengers! The men prefer it that way. In hot weather, when the air conditioning fails, they sit around in their underwear. Feminists are outraged, but the Supreme Court keeps postponing the case. Men's magazines litter the aisles. There are twice as many men's rooms as necessary because there are no ladies' rooms. Once the train screeched to a halt between stations and an alarm sounded. It seems a band of militant women tried to board the train and hijack it. They were eventually beaten back, before the men in the club car even had to put their pants back on.

Le train; masculine.

The French word for "café" is *le café*; masculine. You could either confect another all-male scenario for a café similar to the one you did for the train, or imagine a masculine name emblazoned over the entrance—something like the Macho Café or the Rambo Café.

Le café, masculine.

"Hour" in French is *l'heure*, feminine. Occasionally you get a gift like this one. *Heure* is pronounced very much like *her* without the *r*.

L'heure, feminine.

"Nose" in French is *le nez*, masculine.

The members of which sex break their noses playing football and hockey, boxing, wrestling, and fighting with wise guys who insult their dates?

Le nez, masculine.

"Night" in French is *la nuit*, feminine.

Who ever heard of a "man of the night"?

La nuit, feminine.

"Ticket" in French is *le billet*, masculine.

Always look for opportunities to incorporate a memory book for the gender as you capture the word itself. *Billet* is pronounced *bee-yay*, almost exactly like the letters B.A. as in Bachelor of Arts. If "bachelor" doesn't have a sufficiently strong male connotation to you, imagine a giant male bumble *bee* buzzing around.

Le billet, masculine.

"Train station" in French is *la gare*, feminine.

Shall we imagine women waiting for their homebound commuting husbands at the train station? Not a good idea. You may forget whether the waiting women or the expected husbands are the stars of the association. How about hundreds of women waiting for *one* man, pouncing upon him and fighting over him as he unsuspectingly steps off the train?

La gare, feminine.

"Church" in French is *l'église*, feminine.

Imagine an angry mob of French women storming a church in France, demanding that women be allowed into the Catholic priesthood.

L'église, feminine.

Let this one be a lesson to you. "Mustache" in French is *la moustache*; feminine!

Imagine the circus lady with a mustache, or a new French wine that causes women to grow mustaches, or a little girl asking her mother if she can ever have a mustache.

La moustache; feminine.

Some languages have neuter gender too. Try to come up with associations that suggest icy impersonality.

"House" in German is *das Haus*; neuter.

Imagine a house so cold and unappealing it couldn't have possibly been graced by man *or* woman for years. No one lives there or would ever conceivably want to.

Das Haus; neuter.

"Pen" in Russian is *pero*, pronounced *pee-RAW*. What could be more sexless than a *pea* that's raw?

Pero; neuter.

Reinforcement

You now have a brand new "closet," a foreign-language vocabulary memory system that lets you hang up new words as if they were new clothes. The system just presented will work even better for you if you keep a few tips in mind.

Every example given above is clean in word, deed, and thought. Every one could have been presented from the stage of the Yadkinville, North Carolina, YMCA during Foreign Language Week. I refuse to do any dirty writing, so you have to do some dirty thinking (if you will) to get maximum benefit from the system.

The more vivid, in fact, the more vulgar, your associations are, the more readily they will probably come to mind. Feel free, in your mental imagery, to take clothes off. Get people naked. Get everybody into bed, in the tub, swinging from vines, or making nominating speeches immersed in bubbling Romanian mud. Get them wherever you need them so that the association you want is readily retrievable. X-rated images come readily to mind, even to the minds of nice people. Make your associative images lurid and unforgettable.

We've refrained in our model examples from using names and places to buttress our associations. In a book or a class, we can't. Except for famous figures and places we all know in common, names and places don't mean the same things to everybody. As individuals, however, we can haul off and use any and every proper name we know, whether from our personal lives or from stage, screen, radio, video, song, literature, and legend.

Does the foreign word demand the sound—or any part of the sound—of a *Harry,* an *Edna,* a *Philip,* an *Art,* a *Harold,* a *Doreen,* a *Billy,* a *Lance?* If that name belongs to someone you actually know, your associations will come to you more rapidly and last longer.

Did you grow up around a Reidsville, a Colfax, a Burlington, a Charlotte, a Haw River, or a Mt. Pisgah? Your associations with the foreign words can be enriched by place names that sound like or almost like your target words. You don't actually have to have those places in your biography, so long as you know them and can visualize them and use them as lassos to haul in and hog-tie similar-sounding words. I've never been to Nantucket, but when attacking the Indonesian word for "tired" (*NAN-tuk*), I imagine getting so tired on my initial visit to Nantucket that I collapse into bed exhausted shortly after lunch.

Yet another asset to you is the body of words you already know in another foreign language, or even in the language you're learning. Those who know many languages may conquer a four-syllable word by bringing in sounds from four different languages. This is a classic case of the rich getting richer. Every new word you learn is one more potential hook for grabbing still newer words.

Don't fight to forge a winning association. If at first you don't succeed, try, try again. Then give up! Not all words can be forced into the system, and you're better off not wasting good language-learning time trying to mash an ill-fitting shoe onto Cinderella's sister's foot. Over ninety percent will fit, automatically, neatly, or after some effort. The others, the holdouts, will have to be learned by old familiar rote learning.

Don't forget: make your associations vivid, even if that means making them vulgar.

You'll find that so many truly comical cartoons will dance through your head as you craft your associative images, you'll find yourself constantly having to explain "What's so funny?" to native speakers who wonder what's so hilarious about those ordinary words they're teaching you in their language!

The Plunge

Talk!

Americans feel, with justification, that we're handicapped when it comes to learning other languages. Smaller countries with lots of borders and lots of strange languages on the other side offer more opportunities to absorb other languages than a gigantic United States bounded by the world's two largest oceans and only two land neighbors, the larger one speaking, for the most part, the same language we do.

Admittedly, it's hard to find a Dutchman who doesn't speak four or five languages, a Swiss who doesn't speak at least three, or a Finn, a Belgian, or a Hong Kong Chinese who doesn't speak at least two. Norwegians, Swedes, and Danes subject us to the humiliation of speaking fluent English to each other just to be polite when Americans are present.

Those peoples are not kissed by tongues of flame that render them more intelligent than Americans. They're simply positioned better by geography and history when it comes to acquiring more than one language.

Americans, however, hold one high card that too frequently goes unplayed. We're gregarious. We're extroverts. Some say it contemptuously. Some say it admiringly. But those who

know us best agree that we Americans are the only people in
the world who enjoy speaking another language badly!

The typical European would sooner invite you to inspect
his bedroom fifty seconds after waking up than speak a language he doesn't speak well. Most people in the world are
shy, embarrassed, even paralyzed when it comes to letting
themselves be heard in languages they speak less than fluently. An American may master a foreign language to the point
where he considers himself fluent. A European, however,
who speaks a language equally well and no better will often
deny he speaks it at all!

Give an American a word in another language and he's in
action. Give him a phrase and he's in deeper action. Give him
five phrases and he's dangerous. Take that American trait and
exemplify it.

Talk. Go ahead and talk!

Head into your target language like a moth to the flame,
like a politician to the vote. Is the gentleman you've just been
introduced to from France? And is French the language you
happen to be studying? Then attack.

Don't you dare offer a lame chuckle as you explain in
English that you're trying to learn French but you're sorry,
you're not very good at it yet. That's like giggling and telling
the mugger who ambushes you in an alley that you're learning karate but sorry, you're not very good at it yet.

It's okay to tell him you're just a beginner, but tell him in
French. Learn enough utility phrases in whatever language
you're studying to profit from every encounter. Comb
through your phrase book (the Berlitz *For Travellers* series is
excellent) and make it your priority to master phrases such as
"I don't speak your language well," "Do you understand
me?", "Please speak more slowly," "Please repeat," "How do
you say that in your language?", "Sorry, I don't understand,"
and others that together can serve as your cornerstone and
launching pad.

Most phrase books offer too few of these "crutch" phrases.
When you meet your first encounter, pull out pen and pad

and fatten your crutch collection. Learn how to say things such as, "I'm only a beginner in your language but I'm determined to become fluent," "Do you have enough patience to talk with a foreigner who's trying to learn your language?" "I wonder if I'll ever be as fluent in your language as you are in English," "I wish your language were as easy as your people are polite," and "Where in your country do you think your language is spoken the best?" Roll your own alternatives. You'll soon find yourself developing what comedians call a "routine," a pattern of conversation that actually gives you a feeling of fluency along with the inspiration to nurture that feeling into fruition.

Hauling off and speaking the language you're studying versus merely sitting there knowing it makes the difference between being a business administration professor and a multimillionaire entrepreneur.

It's time to apply the Parable of the Parrot.

A man looking for an anniversary present for his wife after fourteen years of marriage found himself in front of a pet shop. In the window was a parrot, not particularly distinguished in size or plumage, but the price tag on that parrot was a whopping seven thousand dollars because that parrot spoke, unbelievably, fourteen different languages.

That was more than the man intended to spend but he figured, "Fourteen years, fourteen languages!" So he bought it.

He went home, mounted the parrot's perch in the kitchen, and then realized he'd forgotten the birdseed. He ran back to the pet shop, bought the birdseed, and then ran back home, hoping to have everything in readiness before his wife got home.

Alas, she'd already returned, and when he appeared she flung herself upon him in sizzling affection, shouting, "Darling! What a marvelous anniversary present! You remembered how much I love pheasant. I've got him plucked. I've got him slit. I've got him stuffed. He's in the oven and he'll be ready in about fifty minutes."

"You've got him *what*?" cried he. "You've got him *where*? That was no pheasant," stormed the husband. "That was a parrot, and that parrot cost seven thousand dollars because that parrot spoke fourteen different languages."

"So," replied his wife, "why didn't he say something?"

And indeed, why don't you?

Put It in Writing

We don't know if a peacock is impressed when he sees himself in full display in a mirror. We do know that you and I are impressed with ourselves when we behold something we've written in a foreign language.

Try it. If you do nothing more than copy an exercise from your grammar book onto a piece of paper in your own handwriting, you'll enjoy looking at it. You become like a kindergarten child so enraptured with his paint smearings that he can't wait to take them home to Mommy and Daddy.

That's strange, childish, egotistic—and supremely helpful when you're learning another language. Go ahead and write. If you can write letters and cards *to* someone who speaks that language, so much the better. If you can write your dinner preferences for the waiter in an ethnic restaurant, do so. As soon as you feel sufficiently advanced, write a note to the editor of the foreign publication you're learning to read and tell him how helpful it is. Write a letter to the ambassador of a country that speaks your target language and congratulate him on representing a culture sufficiently appealing to make you want to learn his language.

Carry a special little notebook with you at all times so you can jot down your new verbal acquisitions if you happen to meet native speakers of your target language.

As a student of Chinese I used to experience a high energy lift by writing the Chinese characters I'd learned on a blank piece of paper, preferably in red ink. I still get a kick doodling Chinese characters, randomly or in coherent sentences, on the margins of the newspaper I'm carrying or in the blank spaces on the display ads.

Write! Conquer and consolidate by writing. The ability to understand a word when it's spoken or written, to use that word correctly with good pronunciation, and to write it correctly makes you the battlefield commander of that word.

Knowing

Jack Benny was one comic who remained beloved, even by his peers, despite his well-known inability to come up with original material.

Once at a Hollywood roast when another comic laced into him with a devastating salvo that demanded a retort in kind, Benny won the moment by pausing and then saying, "You'd never get away with that if my writers were here."

Cute for Jack Benny at a roast, but not really anything we can borrow. When you're in language action and you stumble and lapse into *uh*s and *ah*s while the native speaker is patiently hoping you'll come through, it doesn't do to say, "I'd never be in this fix if I had my dictionary and phrase book with me."

Everybody who's ever tried to master a foreign language knows the frustration of needing the right word or phrase, knowing that you know it, but being utterly unable to come up with it at the moment. Just as golfers sometimes break their golf clubs in frustration, at some point you'll want to smash your cassette player and throw your books into a shredder. You've mastered a neat set of phrases; they flow glibly off your tongue; you sing them in the shower, repeat them as you dress, review them as you put on your coat—and suddenly all recollection vanishes in a poof when you run into a friend five minutes later who happens to be with a native speaker of the language you're learning and you try to remember how to say "Pleased to meet you."

Having the revolver is one thing. Drawing it quickly is quite another. To take set-piece knowledge you've acquired and have it pop up automatically as instinct under real-game conditions calls for a whole separate discipline.

Coaches stage scrimmages that simulate real-game conditions as closely as possible. Pilots can now train in complex simulators that use some elements of computer games to achieve the effect of genuine flight. You, the language-learner, can play little discipline games that will make your knowledge more readily retrievable in live language action.

First of all, why wait for the real-life foreign-language encounter to spring into retrieval practice? As you go through the motions of daily real life, ask yourself, "What would I be saying here in the language I'm studying?" How would you greet the person headed toward you? What would you say to the friend she introduces you to? How would you thank her? How would you tell her "You're welcome" or not to bother or would she please hand you the fork? It's fun and helpful to dub everyday situations in the language you're learning.

If you come up short in your practice with words and phrases you've already learned, jot them down on a pad and look them up when you get back to your books.

As you review your cassettes, try to come up with the foreign word during the pause before the next piece of English. Put artificial pressure on yourself: "Can I come up with the expression before I hear the next word on the cassette?" Or if you're listening as you're walking, "Can I come up with it before I get to that sign, that lamppost, the corner, the curb?" Victory is being able to take an entire cassette of what were recently nonsense syllables to you and throw back the foreign equivalents without hesitation.

You'll be glad you didn't smash your tools when your friend approaches you by surprise to introduce you to her friend from a country that speaks the language you're learning and you respond with a crisp, correct "Pleased to meet you" in that language!

Commit Language Larceny

There are interesting lessons coiled up inside ordinary greetings in different languages.

The Estonian greeting *Kuidas (käsi käib)* literally means "How does your hand walk?" An old Chinese greeting is *Chr bao le, mei yo?* which means, "Have you had food yet?"—no small achievement in the China of some periods. A charming greeting in Yiddish is *"Zug mir a shtikel Toireh,"* which means, "Teach me a piece of Torah," the Torah being the five books of Moses and the holiest document in the Jewish religion.

Language-learners can use the spirit of that last one to good advantage.

When you encounter a native speaker of your target language, and when you start a conversation in that language, three things are certain. You will be stuck for words you need but don't know. He will use words you don't understand. And you will make mistakes. Get into the habit of exploiting those moments to the hilt!

When you don't know a word, ask him for it. When you don't understand a word he uses, ask him what it means. Ask him to do you the favor of correcting your mistakes. You may not have much luck with that latter request; he may be too polite or too impressed that you're making an effort in his language to criticize you. If you feel he's letting your mistakes slide by, pick a fairly long sentence and ask him to help you hammer out your mistakes in just that one sentence. Write that sentence down on one of your blank flash cards. Ask him to check it again. Milk the moment! As the Latin goes, *Carpe diem!*

Don't ever enter into anything as precious as a conversation in your target language with a native speaker and leave knowing no more than when you started. You've got a repertoire in that language. He has a larger one. Reach in and help yourself.

At No Extra Cost

You may think you have a good idea precisely how your life will improve once you've mastered your target language. You're wrong. It will be much better than you think.

Unexpected good things happen to you when you learn even a little of the other guy's language. A chapter detailing some of those things may seem like preaching to the choir, when you consider that anybody likely to be reading this has already decided he wants to learn. So what? Who more than the members of the choir deserve the inspiration?

All the case histories that follow were culled and corroborated by members of the Language Club who were asked to be alert to all the nice little extras that come your way when you speak another language. Many of them happened to me personally and continue to happen almost daily.

In New York and some other major cities a huge percentage of the cab drivers are from Haiti. Try this, just to get a taste of the power of another language. If your driver is Haitian, lean forward and say (phonetically), "*Sa* (rhymes with "ma") *pass* ("pasta" without the "ta") *SAY* (as in the English "say"), *pa-PA* ("papa," but accented on the last syllable). Sort those sounds out and try it. "*Sa paSAY, paPA?*" It means something like the French *Comment ça va?* ("How are you?"), but it's not French. It's his native Haitian Creole slang and he may never before have heard that utterance from the lips of a non-Haitian.

That one line is guaranteed to get you reactions ranging from a long, slow smile to a cheery "Where did you learn that?" to loud and joyous laughter to the exclamation, "You must know Haiti well!"

Don't get the idea Haitians are the only ones susceptible to the charm of hearing a few words of their language. They just may be more demonstrative than most in showing it. Romanian cab drivers have turned off the meter and given me a free ride in return for my "Good morning" in Romanian.

A Soviet Georgian cab driver refused to take my money and invited me to Sunday dinner at his home, one of the tastiest treats and most interesting evenings I've ever enjoyed. An Indonesian cab driver screamed—that's all, just screamed—upon hearing "Thank you" in his language.

I've long suspected there's a memo posted in the kitchen of every Chinese restaurant in America instructing all personnel not to let any American who exhibits any knowledge of Chinese go unrewarded. Try this experience, just to taste the power.

The Chinese term for "chopsticks" is *kwai dze*. The first word is pronounced like the Asian river the American war prisoners built the bridge over. The second word sounds like the *ds* in "suds."

The next time you're in a Chinese restaurant, smile at the waiter and say, "*Kwai dze.*" When he brings the chopsticks, smile again and says, "*Shieh, shieh*" ("thank you"). Pronounce that as you would "she expects," making sure you never get as far as the *x* and accentuating the "she." The immediate payoffs on this one can range from a free plum brandy cocktail at the end of the meal clear over to a stubborn refusal to let you pay. The more subtle, and satisfying, payoff is that they will assume you know not only the rest of the Chinese language but the Chinese cuisine as well, and they'll probably give you no less than the absolute finest the house can produce every time they see you come in.

Your rewards for knowing even a paltry few words of a language vary in inverse proportion to the likelihood that you'll know any at all. A German baker isn't likely to endorse his whole day's profit on strudel over to your favorite charity merely because you enter his shop with a big "*Guten Tag*" ("Good day"), but an Albanian baker might if you enter with "*Tungjatjeta.*" You won't knock French socks off with a "*Comment allez-vous?*" ("How are you?"), but you may set winter gloves flying in Helsinki with a correctly pronounced "*Hyvää Päivää*" ("Good morning").

Don't overdo it. I've known cab drivers from obscure countries almost drive off the road when they're surprised with a burst of their native tongue from an American passenger, and once I had a Chinese waitress in a Jewish delicatessen (honest!) get so rattled when I ordered for our party in Chinese that she messed up our order beyond redemption.

I have many times ignited what looked like spontaneous street festivals by hailing groups of people on the sidewalk in the language I heard them speaking. They frequently stop, return the greeting, and then start hobnobbing with the people in my group, leading to laughs, the exchange of addresses, dates for later on, and, I suspect, even more! I've never understood the joy of bagging a bird or a deer and watching it fall to the ground. My joy is bagging strangers from other countries with the right greeting in the right language and watching them come to a halt and become old friends at once.

The material payoffs of learning foreign languages are many and predictable, though perhaps a bit surprising in their scope. In early 1990 a friend told me he was looking to fill a job paying $650,000 a year; qualifications: attorney, knowledge of Russian, and willingness to relocate to Moscow. I prefer the psychological payoffs of studying foreign languages— pleasures so keen you could almost call them spiritual.

The joy of a true mathematician escalates as he moves from algebra to trigonometry to calculus. Likewise, the joys of the true language-lover escalates as he advances from what I call "Foreign 1" to "Foreign 2." Foreign 1 is interpreting or translating (interpreters speak, translators write) from your native language to a foreign one. Foreign 2 is doing it from one language that's foreign to you to *another* one that's foreign to you.

You are permitted to feel like Superman when you pull off such a feat. You are not permitted to act like Superman, nor are you permitted to let on that you feel like Superman. Your mien should approximate that of a bored New York commuter telling a stranger how many stops there are between Grand Central Station and New Rochelle.

The best Foreign 2 feeling I ever had was interpreting for Finns trying to communicate with Hungarians. Finnish and Hungarian are widely hailed as the most difficult languages in the world. They're related to each other, but not in any way that's helpful or even apparent. There aren't five words remotely similar in the two languages, and a Hungarian and a Finn can no more understand each other than can a Japanese and a Pole.

I long nurtured a dream of house lights coming up in the theater. The theater manager comes to center stage and says, "Is there a Finnish-Hungarian interpreter in the house?" I wait until he repeats his request louder so that everyone in the theater will get a load of those qualifications. I then, in the fantasy, grudgingly make my presence and, by implication, my suitability for the assignment known. I rise and approach whatever emergency it is that requires my linguistic talents, while those hundreds of theater-goers gasp at their relative inadequacies.

Something like that actually did light up my life for an evening and then some. I was invited by a well-known woman broadcaster to join another couple who had invited her and a guest to a Madison Square Garden horse show. I'd never dated her before. I felt outclassed in the glamour department, and I was uncomfortable as we four wound our way through that upper-crust crowd looking for our places.

Suddenly I was spotted by Anna Sosenko, lyricist, writer, theater producer, and dealer in the memorabilia of show business worldwide and down through the ages. Anna wrote, among other biggies, the song "Darling, Je Vous Aime Beaucoup."

"Hey, Barry," Anna yelled out over the crowd from about twenty rows away. "Can you come by my studio next week? I need you to translate some Ibsen!"

Remember what that sudden spinach infusion did for Popeye's biceps in the animated cartoons? That's exactly what happened to my standing in the foursome after Anna's outcry. My date and her friends turned to me. "Ibsen? You translate Isben? Where did you learn to translate Ibsen?"

They may very well not have known what language Henrik Ibsen wrote in. Never mind! You don't have to be absolutely sure which country a prince is prince of in order to show respect, as long as you're sure he's a real prince. Likewise, with Anna Sosenko doing the yelling, everybody was convinced I could bring Ibsen to life in English.

Motivations

The ads for self-study language courses stress the business, travel, cultural, and literary advantages of acquiring another language. But what about meeting girls? Or women? Or boys? Or men? Why let an old-fashioned propriety quash that thoroughly proper, in fact praiseworthy, reason to learn another language, namely to enlarge your range of social opportunities, to meet people?

Learning another language to enlarge your opportunity for making new connections is fun and rewarding. Financial and professional success have helped people live their dreams. So has learning another language!

There are blonde languages, by the way, and brunette languages. Why be bashful? Those partial to blondes are advised to learn Norwegian, Swedish, Danish, Finnish, German, Dutch, and Hungarian. A good brunette list would include Spanish, French, Portuguese, Italian, Serbo-Croatian, Greek, Turkish, Hebrew, and Arabic.

This advice is not offered flippantly. I find the social motive to learn other languages as valid as the commercial, the cultural, or any other. If your motives for learning another language are social, I would steer you to the language of a people you find maximally attractive with every bit as straight a face as I'd advise those interested in importing from Asia to learn Japanese and opera lovers to learn Italian.

You are not guaranteed love forevermore, but you are guaranteed novelty status. You'll attract attention in your target community as "the one who went to the trouble of learning our language." You'll be invited, introduced around, and questioned thoroughly as to your reasons for studying their particular language. The less popular the language, the greater a celebrity you'll be among its speakers. French is very popular, so you won't have Paris at your feet, we've already agreed, even after your best-rendered "*Comment allez-vous?*" But Norwegians will want to burn arctic moss at your altar when after a meal you say, "*Takk for maten.*" That means "Thanks for the food," which non-Norwegians not only generally don't know how to say, but also don't realize is traditionally said as you leave the table of your host in Norway.

Native English speakers have more to gain from studying other languages than anybody else. Honor, love, cooperation, respect, advantage—they all shower down upon people in inverse proportion to their need to learn a language.

English is the most prominent language in the world. The Dutch, as one example, all seem to know four or five languages well upon graduation from high school, but (I am not trying to diminish their achievement) they *have* to learn other languages, beginning with English, to make their way in the commercial world. You can't play that game with Dutch alone. Languages find their fair rate of exchange as currencies do. We who speak English get a lot more credit from the Dutch if we learn Dutch than they get from us just because they learned English. And so on around the world.

Learn that other language now, while there's still time to enjoy the honors due those who don't *have* to learn the other guy's language but choose to do so anyhow. That time is rapidly running out. For the very first time in our history Americans are learning other languages not out of courtesy but out of necessity. That fact of life is so new it's not yet apparent to

America or the world, so we still have a little more time to bask in the admiration of those who *had* to learn our language and who still believe we simply *chose* to learn theirs.

Something ennobling happens when you learn to communicate in more than one language. And it's fun to watch the magic flash as you touch your word-wand to the ears of those who'd never suspect you speak their language. It's one more way of making friends. In big cities you'll have many chances to find people who speak foreign languages.

But you can't sally in and ambush strangers in their language even if their accent and appearance make it a sure bet. They're probably proud of their accent-free (or nearly accent-free) English. The best way to avoid insulting them—so they can concentrate on loving you when you speak their language—is to say, before you venture one word of their language, "Your accent is beautiful. Are you from England?"

They will then proudly say, "No, I'm from Poland" (or wherever), and they will thereupon welcome your overtures.

Get to Know the Family

Languages have their own happy surprises. For example, Serbo-Croatian and Bulgarian overlap. Learn either one, and at no extra cost you get seventy percent of the other. You may want to select a language to learn according to how much bounce it has beyond its borders. Languages come in families, and it pays to note which relations might work for you.

Let's pursue the Serbo-Croatian–Bulgarian connection. They're related in diminishing degrees to all the Slavic languages, which include Russian, Byelorussian, Polish, Ukrainian, Czech, Slovak, Slovenian, Macedonian, and Ruthenian. They're not all seventy percent overlapping, but so what? What if they're only forty, thirty, twenty percent overlapping? That's still like having the shopkeeper hand you extra cloth on a second bolt when you thought you'd bought only one bolt of cloth.

You learn so much Italian when you learn Spanish that it's a shame not to switch over and pursue Italian once your Spanish is adequate. Portuguese isn't far behind, and even French, the Romance language least like any of the others, has enough similar grammatical features and vocabulary to help you conquer all of the other Romance languages.

Hindi and Urdu, the principal languages of India and Pakistan, are virtually the same spoken language.

Dutch is far more than the language of a tiny nation between Germany and the English Channel. It's almost identical to Flemish, which along with French is one of the two principal languages of Belgium. Dutch is the foundation of Afrikaans, which along with English is a major language of South Africa. And you'll have no trouble finding Dutch speakers all over Indonesia, the old "Spice Islands" ruled by Holland for four hundred years.

Get to know the family of the language you're learning— where it fits in, what other languages it will make easier for you to learn later. What doors in what industries will it open (for example, Flemish and Yiddish for diamonds, Arabic for oil, Swedish for crystal, Italian for fashion)? Over how wide an area is your target language spoken (more Chinese speak Chinese outside China than Frenchmen speak French in France)? Knowing where your language fits into the world mosaic will offer you countless advantages and rewards, and almost certainly the motivation to learn more.

Language Power to the People

The many who crave language knowledge in America have risen in rebellion against the many who have failed (we could even say *refused*) to give it.

Language teaching used to be in the control of "the faculty," a Prussian guard of grammarians who taught that after all the conjugations, declensions, irregularities, and exceptions were mastered, surely fluency would follow. What followed instead was a parade of hapless Americans who, after eight years of good grades, could not go to the desk clerk at a hotel in a country whose language they'd studied and ask if they had any messages!

"The faculty" taught rigidly by the book, the grammar book, and all our desire to learn to say useful things and converse were dashed.

Today foreign languages are no longer "electives." Those suddenly faced with their first need to command another language are besieging Berlitz and other commercial language schools and buying the Pimsleur cassettes and other self-study courses. We the laymen are picking up our tools—language workbooks, cassette courses, phrase books, flash cards—to try to make up for our failure to learn, while all those incredible Europeans were learning English in their public schools!

Two, four, six, eight years of high-school and college study in a foreign language, and still our American graduates can't tell whether the man on the radio speaking the language they "learned" is declaring war or recommending a restaurant!

Has one single American graduate ever stepped into a job that called for a foreign language with nothing more than the language he learned in high school or college? It's not a cruel question. Most Americans can get by on the reading they learned in school. And the math. And the history. Why is it that when it comes to foreign languages our graduates have to rush into expensive private instruction to start all over again?

One hero of language learning in the United States is Dr. Henry Urbanski, professor of Russian, former chairman of the Department of Foreign Languages of the State University of New York at New Paltz, and now director of the Language Immersion Institute. Once upon a time Dr. Urbanski's "immersion" heresy would have probably have resulted in his getting banned from university life. Today Urbanski is showered with praise and honor.

His immersion program defies the language-teaching tradition of rote regimentation and grammar worship. There are no charts to learn, no homework, no drudgery, and no tests. It's all fun, it emphasizes real conversation between teacher and students, and it all takes place over a weekend. If Henry Urbanski could have thought of any more rules to break, he would have.

Urbanski's immersion program is open to everybody. Those with no educational background in languages whatever join with people with graduate degrees in languages and men and women of all levels of qualifications in between. The program begins at seven P.M. on a Friday for an hour of introduction and orientation. The students then break up into small groups in separate rooms and jump into the foreign language under the command of dynamic, enthusiastic instructors who keep a high-energy Ping-Pong of basic conversation going back and forth with all students participating. At ten P.M. Friday the classes break and the wise ones go straight to bed without food, wine, or small talk, knowing that the routine resumes early Saturday morning.

Even when classes break for lunch Saturday afternoon there's no break in the language. The various groups have lunch together in the language they're learning. Then they return to class and keep on going.

On Saturday at dusk some of the students begin to report phenomena resembling out-of-body experiences. Urbanski jokes, "Only when this constant bombardment collapses your resistance can the new language come surging in like an angry sea through a broken dike."

Even the students who were suggesting wine and talk the night before hasten to bed in order to meet the dawn on Sunday, the final day. Sessions continue clear up to a late lunch, after which there's a "graduation" exercise, whereupon everybody vows to return at the next opportunity for immersion in the next highest level of their language.

Dr. Urbanski wants his immersion students to have fun. Walk down the corridors during teaching hours (or follow a group on a "language hike" through the mountains around New Paltz) and you'll hear laughter, clapping, singing, and what sound like pep rallies in Spanish, French, German, Italian, Russian, and the other languages of the weekend.

"Why make students suffer unnecessarily?" Urbanski asks. "Learning a language doesn't have to bring pain and suffering. We believe in providing a nonthreatening environment in which students are rewarded for their progress but not punished for their errors." An immersion graduate added, "The festival spirit wakes us up, keeps us sharp, lubricates the flow of new words, and anesthetizes us against the pain of grammar."

Urbanski never promises you can go straight from a weekend of foreign-language immersion to a booth at the United Nations and simultaneously interpret a foreign minister's address. What immersion promises is a more than elementary introduction to the language, a good grounding in its words and melodies, the ability to "defend" yourself in that language without help, and a solid base from which you can grow, either through self-study or more courses. No claim is made that students will be fluent by the end of one immersion weekend. "We teach linguistic survival," says Urbanski. "After a few immersion weekends our students can manage in the language."

The New Paltz Language Immersion Institute has grown from immersion weekends on campus to weekends at the nearby Mohonk Mountain House resort and in Manhattan. A program is now under way in Washington, D.C. Anyone desiring information—no qualifications necessary—may call the New Paltz Language Immersion Institute at 1-800-LANGUAGE.

Tuition for the weekend ranges from $175 to $250, depending on location. The two-week summer program at the New Paltz campus costs $400.

In the words of one satisfied institute graduate, "I learned enough to continue to learn more!"

Back to Basics

"Send the manager to this table immediately," demanded the diner in the restaurant. When the manager appeared, the diner railed, "This is the worst vanilla ice cream I've ever had."

"I'm sorry, sir," said the manager. "That's not vanilla ice cream. That's butter pecan."

"Oh," said the customer, suddenly placated. "For butter pecan, it's okay."

This chapter on the basics of grammar should be read in that spirit.

"French verb changes are inaudible through the singular of the present tense."

"The Spanish auxiliary verb 'to have' is completely different from the verb 'to have' implying possession."

"The Scandinavian languages, Romanian, and Albanian are among the languages that place the definitive article after the noun."

"Chinese has no case endings or verb inflections, and adjectives do not have to agree with nouns."

Do you understand all of the above, or most of it? If so, you don't need this chapter, though some of it might come as a welcome refresher. This chapter is offered as catch-up for all of you

117

who didn't pay attention in English class. Now you want to learn another language and you realize suddenly that your teacher was right, you were wrong, and here you are unable to understand the English you need to take command of another language.

I, like you, sat smugly through grade-school English convinced that ignorance of all those silly terms that went zipping by me would never interfere with any of my future endeavors. Nothing reforms the student who's apathetic toward English like a sudden desire to learn other languages. I could have learned foreign languages more easily from the outset had I sat down to learn just these bare bones I serve you now.

What follows is a rundown of some of the terms you'll need to know to advance easily through another language. The synopsis may be misprioritized and incomplete, but on the other hand it is friendly, nonjudgmental, brief, blunt, and, I hope, helpful.

NOUN

A noun is a person, place, or thing—either a tangible thing, like a block of ice or a head of cattle or your mother-in-law, or an intangible thing, like a concept or an emotion.

PRONOUN

The dictionary tells us that pronouns are words that serve as substitutes for nouns. If that's confusing, ignore it and let's get right down to the pronouns. In English they are *I, you, he, she, it, we, they, me, him, her, us, them, my, mine, your, yours, his, hers, its, our, ours, their,* and *theirs*.

In addition, we have INTERROGATIVE pronouns (who, what, which), for asking questions.

We also have RELATIVE pronouns (who, whose, which, that) for explaining and describing the nouns we use.

In the sentence "*Who* owns that house?" the pronoun *who* is used in its interrogative form. It's asking a question. In the sentence "The man *who* owns that house is nice," the pronoun *who* is used in its relative sense. You're not asking anybody a question, you're identifying the man. "The man *whose* house . . . ," "The house, *which* I visited . . . ," and "The house *that* I visited . . ." all demonstrate the use of relative pronouns.

VERB

A verb is an action word— *to do, to go, to want, to think.* Chances are that any word that sounds right after the word *to* (provided the *to* doesn't mean "toward" or "in the direction of") is a verb. English verbs are so consistent (unchanging), it's easy for the English speaker to get overwhelmed when tackling a language whose verbs INFLECT (change forms), as all the Romance, the Slavic, and many other languages' verbs do. When we follow a verb through all its forms (*I go, you go, he goes, we go, they go,* in the present tense, past tense, future tense, etc.) we are CONJUGATING that verb. You'll feel less bewildered if you stop to realize that our own English verbs inflect just enough to give you the idea of changing forms. The present tense, third-person singular form of the English verb (the *he* form) usually adds an *s* (*I give, you give,* but *he gives*).

INFINITIVE

An infinitive is a verb in neutral gear. In English the infinitive is the form we talked about above— *to go, to do,* etc. The infinitive form of the verb *go* is therefore *to go.* That doesn't tell you who's going or when he's going or, in case he's already gone, when he went. The infinitive is just hanging there, ready to express any and all of the above possibilities when the proper INFLECTIONS, changes, are applied.

The gears that neutral infinitives can shift into involve PERSON, NUMBER, and TENSE. We'll tackle them in that order.

PERSON

I am FIRST PERSON. *You* are SECOND PERSON. *He, she,* or *it* is THIRD PERSON. The fussbudget grammarian wants to blow the whistle right here and remind us that *we, you,* and *they* are also first, second, and third person. Don't rush me. We're getting to it.

NUMBER

Number, in English and most other languages, is either SINGULAR or PLURAL. (In Russian and other Slavic languages there's a third one. They have singular, plural, and *really* plural. Be grateful!) *I,* the first person, am only one individual. Therefore I am first-person singular. *You,* by yourself, are second-person singular. *He, she,* and *it* are third-person singular.

We is more than one person; therefore *we* is first-person plural. *You,* meaning two or more of you, is second-person plural. Second-person singular and second-person plural in English happen to look and sound identical. That's not so in all languages. *They* is third-person plural. The one English word *they* covers as many *he's, she's* and *it's* as anybody can possibly throw at you. Again, not all languages are so obliging!

TENSES

Even those who didn't pay much attention in school shouldn't have difficulty with tenses. *I am* is PRESENT tense. (To give it its full name and rank we'd have to say *I am* is the present-tense, first-person singular of the verb *to be.*)

You were is PAST tense or, more fully, the past-tense, second-person singular (in this case it could be plural too) of the verb *to be.*

He will be is FUTURE tense, or the future-tense, third-person singular of the verb *to be.*

The PERFECT tense is another form of the past tense that expresses not *I was* but rather *I have been.* (*Perfect* here just means "finished.") This tense is more important in English than in many other languages, and more important in French than in English.

The PAST PERFECT (also called PLUPERFECT) tense is *I had been*. It takes place before the "regular" past.

The IMPERFECT ("unfinished") tense is *I was being, I was walking, I was going, doing,* etc.

The CONDITIONAL tense is *I would be.*

There are more tenses, and they may vary from language to language, but that's enough to give you the hang of what tenses are.

AUXILIARIES

As the name suggests, auxiliaries are words that help you accomplish something. In English, the verb *to have* serves as the auxiliary that helps us form the perfect tenses (*I have been, I had been*). The verb *to be* serves as the auxiliary that helps us form the imperfect tense (*I was going*).

NOUN CASES

Just as ice, water, and steam are merely different forms of the same thing, *I, me, my,* and *mine* are merely different forms of the same word. You pick the form according to what CASE you need. (Yes! You already do this in English.) Let's advance on case now and destroy its mystery before it destroys your enthusiasm.

Noun (and pronoun) cases turn more people away from learning languages than boot camp turns away from joining the marines. And the same reason underlies both. Those who've been there enjoy boosting their own glory by exaggerating the difficulties involved to the intimidated uninitiated.

"Wait until those drill instructors at Parris Island get a hold of you!" is essentially the same comment as "Wait until you run into all those noun cases!" You may recall with distaste the trouble you had with Latin's six noun cases. Russian also has six noun cases. Serbo-Croatian has seven. Other languages have even more.

Anyone studying a language bristling with noun cases knows the sinking feeling of leaving warm, shallow water and running into wave after wave of charts showing nouns that change their endings for no apparent reason!

You can ride those waves. Those nouns, in fact, change for very good reasons, reasons that are easy to catch on to provided you're not laboring under the spell of a show-off know-it-all who tells you, "Finnish! Forget it. They have fifteen noun cases in the singular and sixteen in the plural!"

Fortunately, English has just enough of what we call noun cases to prove they're nothing to fear.

Let's play with the word *house*. "The *house* is large." "The exterior of the *house* is green." "Let's go to the *house*." "I see the *house*." In all of those sentences, the form of *house* remains mercifully (for anybody learning English) the same. If there were any reason to strain a point and prove that plain English nouns can have case too, we could confect the sentence, "The *house's* exterior is green," and point out that *house's* is the genitive case of *house*.

To get a fuller example of case, we have to go to our English pronouns. "*I* have a pen." "*My* pen is good." "Give the pen to *me*." "Do you hear *me*?"

Look what happened to *I* as it changed roles in the various sentences. In the sentence "*I* have a pen," *I* is the subject of the sentence. In the sentence "*My* pen is good," *I* has changed to *my* to express the concept of possession. In the sentence "Give the pen to *me*," *I* becomes the indirect object of the giving, and in the sentence "Do you hear *me*?" *I* becomes the direct object of the verb *hear*.

If I wanted to discourage you instead of inspire you, I would say, "We have now met the NOMINATIVE case, the GENITIVE case, the DATIVE case, and the ACCUSATIVE case, and we're all going to stay right here and not come up for air until you can decline (give me the lineup) of 189 nouns in all those cases in the language you'd like to learn!" Instead I say let's move forward and learn how to say things and read things and understand things in the language. You can learn about noun cases and other grammatical complexities exactly the way you learned from your uncles and aunts when you were a baby—one hug, one kiss, one lollipop at a time.

When we carry the noun through all its cases we say we're DECLINING that noun. Noun cases tip you off to the role of the noun or pronoun in a sentence. Many languages need them to tell you who is doing what to whom. Approach them with a good attitude and you will feel the wisdom of Mark Twain's little sermon, "Fear knocked at the door. Faith answered. No one was there."

ADJECTIVES

Adjectives are words that describe nouns. In the phrase "the green pen," *green* is the adjective that describes *pen*. You'll encounter some fuss about them because in many languages adjectives have to AGREE WITH (appear in the same form as) the nouns they MODIFY (refer to). In those languages adjectives must agree with the nouns in gender and number (and sometimes case).

A little Spanish will quickly make it clear. *El libro es rojo* ("The book is red") shows the adjective *rojo* ("red") in masculine singular form to agree with *libro* ("book"). *La pluma es roja* ("The pen is red") shows the adjective *roja* ("red") in feminine singular form to agree with *pluma* ("pen"). *Los libros son rojos* ("The books are red") shows the adjective *rojos* ("red") in masculine plural form to agree with *libros* ("books"). And finally, *Las plumas son rojas* ("The pens are red") shows the adjective *rojas* ("red") in feminine plural forms to agree with *plumas* ("pens").

ADVERBS

Adverbs describe verbs—they tell *how*. "He mastered the easy parts of the language *easily.*" *Easily* is the adverb telling *how* he mastered the easy parts. (*Easy*, of course, is the adjective.)

PREPOSITIONS

Prepositions are words that precede nouns and pronouns to form phrases (groups of words) that can act as adjectives or adverbs. Prepositions show relationships among nouns; they often indicate position or direction, and they are often short words: *to, at, by, for, with, from, toward, on, over, behind, between,* etc.

DEFINITE ARTICLE

The definite article in English is the word *the*.

INDEFINITE ARTICLE

The indefinite article in English is the word *a* or *an*. English has both the definite and the indefinite article. Some other languages also have both. Some have one but not the other. Some have neither.

SUBJECT-VERB-OBJECT

Words like these symbolize the grade-school "nerve gas" which deadens the desire to proceed through grammar and parts of speech, and diagramming sentences, and all related yawn-provokers that once seemed to float too far over our heads ever to zoom down and give us discomfort. Those concepts may have seemed like distant enemies in the eighth grade when you had no intention of becoming an English teacher, but they're close friends and necessary allies when you're learning another language.

Briefly, in the sentence "He hits the ball," the word *he* is the SUBJECT, *hits* is the VERB, *ball* is the OBJECT, the DIRECT OBJECT. If we lengthen the sentence to "He hits the ball to him," then *him* is the INDIRECT OBJECT.

ACTIVE

The verb is ACTIVE or in the ACTIVE VOICE if the subject is performing the verb action. In "He hits the ball," the verb *hits* is in the active voice because the subject *he* is the one (the AGENT) doing the hitting.

PASSIVE

The verb is PASSIVE or in the PASSIVE VOICE if the subject receives or is subject to the action of the verb. Thus in "The ball is hit by him," the subject *ball* doesn't do any hitting. Rather, it gets hit. Therefore we say that the verb *hit* is in the passive voice because the subject *ball* is not performing the action of the verb but is rather having that action performed upon it.

REFLEXIVE

The verb is reflexive when its action bounces back upon itself. In the sentence "I dress myself," the subject *I* both performs the action and has it performed on itself.

IMPERATIVE

The imperative is the command form of the verb. The imperative of the verb *to go* is *Go!* The imperative of the verb *to watch* is *Watch!*

COMPARATIVE AND SUPERLATIVE

Though not as flighty and volatile as verbs and nouns, English adjectives and adverbs can't sit entirely still.

Good, better, and *best* are really the same word in escalating degrees. *Good* is the simple, the base form of the adjective. *Better* is the comparative form. *Best* is the superlative form.

Good-better-best is an example of an irregular comparative-superlative construction. If it were regular, it would be *good, gooder,* and *goodest,* like the regular *neat, neater, neatest.*

The comparative and superlative of adverbs in English is formed with *more* and *most:* "He progressed *rapidly.* He progressed *more rapidly.* He progressed *most rapidly.*"

CARDINAL AND ORDINAL NUMBERS

Cardinal numbers are *one, two, three, four,* etc. Ordinal numbers are *first, second, third, fourth,* etc.

FORMS OF ADDRESSES

English is deceptively easy in forms of address. Everybody in second-person singular and plural is *you.* Your spouse is *you.* Your four-year-old child is *you.* Your interior decorator is *you.* The President of the United States is *you.* Your cocker spaniel is *you.* In almost every other language, speakers differentiate, sometimes sharply, between the FAMILIAR form of address (French *tu,* German *du*) and the FORMAL form (French *vous,* German *Sie*). The usual rule is that you use the familiar form of address only when addressing (talking to) intimates, children, and animals. All others take the formal form.

There comes a moment in the affairs of humans when someone who started out formally as a stranger or casual acquaintance becomes, with time and congeniality, so familiar that the formal form of address seems almost stilted and even offish or insulting. In some countries—Norway, for instance—the tension is broken by the suggestion *Skal vi drikke dus?* ("Shall we drink to a new era in our friendship?" one in which we'll address each other as the familiar *du* rather than the formal *De?*) That's a speak-now-or-forever-hold-your-peace moment in the relationship. If there's no objection, the two friends take a glass and toast their graduation from formal to familiar with their drinking arms intertwined!

DIMINUTIVES

A charming trick almost every language has is the "shrinking" of someone or something you like by the use of diminutives. The diminutive of *Charles* is *Charlie*. The diminutive of *William* is *Billy*. The diminutive of *star* is *starlet*. The diminutive of *pig* is *piglet* or *piggy*. The Olympics of diminutives is won hands-down by the Italians, who have literally dozens of different forms of the diminutive, each conveying its own special nuance of feeling for the noun undergoing the shrinking.

IDIOMS

Idioms are expressions that may not make sense but have clear and specific meaning anyhow because the speakers of the language have "agreed" that, rules notwithstanding, those particular words shall have a particular meaning. An idiom has a meaning that cannot be derived from the conjoined meanings of its elements.

In English we say, "Let's *take* a walk!" What are you *taking*? In Spanish that becomes *"Damos un paseo,"* which literally means "Let's *give* a walk!" What are you *giving*? Neither makes much sense but both are correct. Both are idioms.

Some English idioms, at random, are: *at first blush, at one's wits end, ax to grind, beat around the bush, break the ice, chip off the old block, crack a joke, fit as a fiddle, forty winks, get in one's hair, give a piece of one's mind, keep the wolf from the door, red tape,* and *with flying colors.*

All languages have idioms. They're fun and enriching and they illustrate differences *and* similarities among cultures. How philosophically distant is the Norwegian who says about a dim-witted person, *"Han er darlig utstyrt i oeverst etasje"* ("He's poorly equipped on the top floor"), from the American Southerner who says, "He's three pickles shy of a barrel"?

Learn to diagnose idioms in English and make sure you never try to translate them literally into any other language. If you try to tell a Spanish friend, "I'm on a roll," do not say, *"Estoy en un panecillo."* He will look under your feet for signs of crumbs without any comprehension that what you really meant to express is that things are going extremely well for you at the moment.

Likewise, be attentive to idioms as they come at you in other languages. The German who tells you to "break your neck and your leg" is really wishing you luck. So is the Italian who seems to be sending you "into the mouth of the wolf"!

The foregoing is by no means the whole of the mechanical vocabulary you'll need to conquer every other language on earth. You've got some dandies waiting for you inside whatever language you choose to tackle. In French and other languages you'll meet the double negative. In Finnish, it's worse: you'll meet the *inflecting* negative! German will be watching to see if you can handle its double infinitive. Russian can't wait to hit you with its perfective and imperfective verb aspects. Gender in Hebrew is so complex you have to know the sex of a dog before you can command it to quit biting you.

These are not monsters in the woods. The lovely people who speak all those languages descend from people who found every single one of those Bermuda Triangles of grammar utterly logical and useful, and they've never felt the need to change.

The old school grammarians, the ones who assassinated the desire of young Americans to learn foreign languages, were right in their insistence that knowledge of grammar is vital.

They were wrong, however, to insist that all grammar must be learned here and now before we take our first step into conversation and the fun of learning another language.

Again, grammar is best attacked from the rear. When you read the rule in your grammar book you may say to yourself, "Oh, so *that's* the reason I've been saying it that way all along, the way I learned from my phrase book, my cassettes, my newspaper, and my Italian friend at the pizzeria!"

When you come upon an explanation of a grammatical wrinkle and you don't understand all the terms in English, pick up a dictionary (not a language dictionary, but an English-only dictionary). You've got to know something of your own language before you can efficiently learn another.

Last Words Before the Wedding

It is my hope that this volume will help those who've never yet dared to make the commitment, march to the altar, and "marry" another language. If you've already studied other languages, perhaps tried for years with disappointing results, let's look at your next effort as a second marriage, fortified, this time, with the foregoing advice.

Best men and bridesmaids traditionally utter inanities to grooms and brides before they march down the aisle. As your avuncular advisor, who at this writing has studied foreign languages as a hobby for forty-six years, let me use this precious final opportunity to hammer home some points—some repeats and some leftovers—that will ensure your success and ensure that you enjoy yourself as you succeed.

Plunge In

When an interviewer asked the famed bank robber Willy Sutton why he robbed banks, he replied, "Because that's where the money is." Using the language is where the real learning is. There's a direct analogy to sports and war. Ask any ball player to give his views on the difference between watching the coach diagram plays on a blackboard and facing the opponents in a real game. Ask any soldier the difference between basic training and actual combat.

That same difference exists between language study and language use. Try recalling the words and phrases you've learned most recently the next time you meet by surprise a speaker of the language. Your mind is likely to be a frustrating blank. Once you've used your knowledge in real life, however, your chances of recall are much greater.

Go out, then, and "pick" conversations in the language you're learning, like a belligerent drunk picks fights.

Certain words, phrases, idioms, and grammatical constructions will remain unmeltable lumps. They will defeat your best efforts to learn them. Many students accept such unscalable heights as proof that "I don't have an ear for languages!" (That, by the way, is the most pernicious myth of all. If you have the motivation and discipline to proceed through the system, it doesn't matter what kind of "ear" you have, so long as it can hear.)

Once you score your first victory over one of those "unconquerable" fortresses, an emotional momentum is released that will carry you forward. Grab hold of the nearest holdout word and beat the hell out of it. Bite at it one syllable at a time or even one letter at a time. Throw fits of irrational energy against it until it's yours.

There is something truly serene about encountering a word that used to be a hideous holdout—and is now as familiar to you as your middle name!

Point of sale is too good a term to be limited to disposable razors and other sundries arrayed near the cash register at convenience stores. Let's apply it to getting ahead in a foreign language.

The quickest and easiest time I ever had learning a phrase in a foreign language was *Molim za ples,* which is Serbo-Croatian for "May I have this dance?" I was a college student visiting

Yugoslavia. An unforgivably attractive young woman smiled at me across the gym floor at a student dance. I asked Darko, my interpreter companion, how to say, "May I have this dance?"

"Molim za ples," he replied.

I had no idea whether the *mo* or the *lim* or the *za* or the *ples* meant "May" or "I" or "have" or "this" or "dance." Nor did I waste time worrying about it. I simply strode across the floor, said *"Molim za ples,"* and enjoyed my first dance in Yugoslavia!

Darko was giving me point-of-sale instruction.

Use it! When you know you're going to a restaurant the day after tomorrow where the waiters speak the language you're trying to learn, don't use your hidden moments in the meantime on general vocabulary. Sit down and compile a restaurant vocabulary of food items and utensils and let that be your focus from that moment until you leave the restaurant after the meal.

Are you headed for a party over the weekend where you're fairly sure at least one guest speaks your target language? Start carrying your phrase book as well as your flash cards and review the "getting to know you" phrases, such as "Where are you from?" "How long do you intend to stay in America?" etc.

Whenever you see an impending opportunity to speak the language, get a head start by sizing up the news of the day and going into your dictionary for the terms you'll need that you don't yet know. ("Election," "proposal," "tariff," "amend," "hostage," "coup," etc.) Focus your learning effort opportunistically to make the best possible showing when you reach the point of sale—the conversation you can anticipate.

The "show," by the way, is not to impress others. It's to impress that part of you that, when you hear yourself doing so well, will inspire you to proceed with your broad-front general advance through the language.

A policeman is a policeman twenty-four hours a day. So is a fireman, a spy, a marine, and a language-learner. Learn to catch yourself several times a day, indoors or outdoors, and look around. What are the first five things you see that you don't know how to say in your target language? Write the English down on a blank flash card and fill in the target language words when you get home to your dictionary.

At least once a day pretend you're a United Nations interpreter simultaneously interpreting what somebody is saying to you in your target language. When he gets to the fifth word that you wouldn't know how to say in your target language, abandon the exercise and write those words down, again, on a blank flash card. Fill in the foreign side of the flash card as soon as you get back to your dictionary.

Reward-and-Denial Games

This is a clever way to speed learning. Impose little discipline games on yourself geared to bringing you back to the language often throughout the day for short periods that can't possibly get in your way. Don't let yourself have the first cup of coffee until you review ten of the words you learned yesterday. Permit yourself dessert if you can go through ten whole flash cards without a mistake. Say yes to the extra glass of wine if you can name any five objects in the room in the foreign language while you hold your breath. Let yourself take off and go see the movie once you're able to beat the speaker on the cassette to the foreign word or phrase for a solid minute. Or, as you advance, two or three minutes.

Roll your own rules. It's painless. It's fun. It's character-building. And it rushes you forward to quicker results.

Profanity and Vulgarity

Forget it. Whoever uses foul language even in English among people he doesn't know well loses standing. When you go out of your way to use bad language in a foreign language, it's much worse.

One night in a blockhouse on the Austrian side of the Hungarian border waiting for refugees to come across, our all-male crowd represented three languages: English, German, and Hungarian. A brisk discussion in comparative obscenity broke out and a fascinating pattern emerged. Whatever we had three or four dirty words for in English, German always had sixteen or seventeen and Hungarian never less than thirty-five!

Sure, the other guy's garbage is fun to know, but it's tacky, so leave it alone. It's all right to get command of their unacceptable terms for defensive purposes only—so you'll know what *not* to say and be able to exercise caution when using words dangerously similar to the no-no words.

It's a good idea to follow Maimonides on this one: "What is lofty may be said in any language. What is mean should be said in none."

Your Second Foreign Language, Your Third, and So On

It's said that once you master one foreign language, all others come much more easily. That's not a myth. Your first foreign language, in a major way, is the first olive dislodged from the bottle. The rest flow obligingly forth.

Moreover, your second foreign language need have no connection to your first. Chinese will be easier if you've first mastered Italian. Greek will be easier if you've mastered Japanese. You pick up the principles of how language works with your first conquest. I once asked a man who commanded easily a dozen languages how he did it.

"I started out studying languages when I was young," he said, "and I was just too lazy to quit!"

He was kidding, of course, but a lot of true words are spoken through exaggerations.

The Right Word

Don't settle for being merely understood. Some of the least intelligent and most unspectacular people on earth can be understood in languages other than their own. Keep pressing forward toward perfection. "He thinks he's a big shot" gets the notion across, but that shouldn't satisfy the learner of English searching for the word "megalomaniac."

It's a marvelous feeling of unfolding and growth when you learn more and more words that take you closer and closer to the bull's-eye of what you want to express.

Saying It Right

One of the most maddening things about language learning — you'll encounter it time and again — is having the face of the native you're speaking with suddenly go blank. You've used a word he doesn't understand. He asks you to repeat it. You do. He still doesn't understand. You repeat it again. Slower. Louder. Finally, in frustration, desperation, and humiliation, you write the word down or show it to him in your book.

Then he gets it. "Ahh," the native speaker says, the black night of your spoken error suddenly pierced by the flashbulb of print. And then — here's the payoff — he proceeds to repeat exactly what you've been saying to him a dozen or so times without his comprehending!

That syndrome is particularly prevalent in Chinese, though you risk in it every language. Be a sport. Eat crow. And even though you're far from the mood at that moment, try to catch something in what he says that's at least slightly different from what you've been saying. If the next native speaker understands your revised pronunciation without an argument, then that crow you were forced to eat will retroactively taste like pheasant!

Every language student has bad days and good days with the language for no apparent reason. On bad days you can't seem to unleash a simple greeting without monumental phumphering. On good days you actually feel supernaturally propelled. A rising tide lifts all boats. Keep working. The bad days as well as the good days will both be better.

To Speak or Not to Speak

Be neither too boorish nor too reticent with your new knowledge. Don't go barreling in with scant command of a language if doing so causes ungainly delays in a busy restaurant. Neither should you let shyness deny you a good opportunity to send a few volleys of conversation across the net.

Don't be like the beginner who took his party into a French restaurant in New York and insisted on trying to order for everybody in French. The waiter, himself French, quickly abandoning any hope of understanding the poor wretch, pulled a diplomatic coup worthy of a medal and a kiss on both cheeks.

"I'm sorry," he said, with an accent French enough to draw the truffles up out of the underbrush of Alsace, "I don't speak French."

"You don't speak French!" thundered the hapless show-off.

"Non, monsieur," said the waiter.

"Well, then," said he, "send me somebody who does!"

Speaking of Peace

Does knowledge of other languages lead to peace? One witness says, "No. Knowing the other guy's language merely enables you to get into more arguments of greater depth and intensity." Another witness says, "Of course, language knowledge breeds peace. How could I pull a trigger and shoot a man when what I really want is a chance to sit down with him and learn his irregular verbs?" Put me solidly in the latter category. It's impossible to learn a language and not learn a great deal about the country and its people. And usually those who learn about a country and its people develop a certain empathy and advocacy for that nation.

When Serb fights Croat in Yugoslavia, I don't ignore it. Neither do I choose sides. They were both so helpful to me when I was learning Serbo-Croatian. I want them all to work together and get along.

A little knowledge of a language, then of a people, can convert even a rabid partisan into a one-man peace movement!

Keep Learning

Stay with it. Keep pressing ahead with all tools in all the ways suggested, plus whatever other ways you discover en route that seem to work for you. Keep pursuing opportunities to use what you learn, not just in exercises and self-simulation, but in genuine, real-life conversation, reading, writing, and comprehension.

When will you "arrive"? When will you no longer "be studying" but "have learned" the language?

Never! At least, pretend never. Your linguistic infancy will lead to babyhood, childhood, adolescence, young adulthood— and so on. Your fragments of knowledge will lead to competence. Your competence will lead to fluency. Your fluency will intensify to higher and higher levels of fluency.

The best attitude, however, is that your attempt to master the foreign language, should remain perpetually unfinished business.

You'll succeed if you make sure you never go to bed knowing no more of your target language than you did when you woke up!

PART THREE

Appendixes

The Language Club

In 1984 some of us language-lovers decided that, although there were plenty of places in New York to *learn* foreign languages, there were no places to go to *practice* foreign languages.

Sure, you can let fly a greeting in Italian and a request for red pepper at the pizzeria and practice similar performances at even the busiest French restaurant, but there was no place to sit down, have a glass of wine, open books, converse with others, and consult with native speakers for two or three hours at a time.

So we started the Language Club with "practice parties" every Monday night at La Maganette, a restaurant in Manhattan at the corner of Third Avenue and Fiftieth Street. That remains our "mother club," though we've extended our practice parties to other evenings and other restaurants—even a Sunday brunch at Victor's on Columbus Avenue at Seventy-first Street.

Our mission is to enable men and women to practice conversation in other languages in a pleasant, non-threatening atmosphere at fine restaurants at a minimum price. The restaurants understand the uniqueness of the Language Club and enjoy catering to such a high-minded endeavor.

The questions callers most frequently ask about the Language Club are "What night is French?" and "What's your age group?"

We explain that *every* night is French night—all languages are welcome at all practice parties. When you enter you go to the French table, the Italian table, the Spanish table, the German table, the Russian table, etc. Many visitors grasshopper from table to table, practicing three, four, or more different languages at the same practice party.

When they ask about age group, we immediately understand that their agenda is broader than mere language practice! We first explain we're a *language* club, not a "social" club or a "singles" club. We emphasize that age is irrelevant, since someone five years old can provide good language practice for someone ninety-five years old.

Having made that point, we then relent a bit and explain that indeed many of our members are single, and if two single language-lovers should enter our practice party separately and leave together, we don't blow a whistle and pull a citizen's arrest. In fact, we have several "language marriages" to our credit and at least one confirmed birth!

All we ask is your sincere interest in language practice. All your other interests will be tolerated provided they do not result in any infringement of the law!

All those wishing more information about the Language Club may write:

> The Language Club
> P.O. Box 121
> New York, NY 10108

Our telephone number is (212) 787-2110.

The Language Club has no official club handshake, club song, club motto, or club dues. (You come when you feel like it and pay for your own meal.)

We do, however, have an official club joke. Once you know this joke, you're as much a member of the Language Club as anybody else.

Two mice were hopelessly trapped. A hungry cat was poised to pounce. There was no escape.

At that last instant, one of the mice put his little paws up to his lips and yelled, "Bow-wow!"

The cat turned around and ran away.

Whereupon that mouse turned to the other mouse and said, "You see, that's *the advantage* of knowing a second language!"

The Principal Languages of the World

Source: Sidney S. Culbert, University of Washington, Seattle, Wash. 98195

Total number of speakers (native plus nonnative) of languages spoken by at least one million persons (midyear 1989)

Language	Millions
Achinese (N. Sumatra, Indonesia)	3
Afrikaans (South Africa)	10
Akan (or Twi-Fante) Ghana	7
Albanian (Albania; Yugoslavia)	5
Amharic (Ethiopia)	17
Arabic	197
Armenian (USSR)	5
Assamese (Assam, India; Bangladesh)	22
Aymara (Bolivia; Peru)	2
Azerbaijani (Iran; USSR)	14
Balinese (Indonesia)	3
Baluchi (Bakuchistan, Pakistan)	4
Bashkir (USSR)	1

Batak Toda (including Anakola) Indonesia
(see also Karo-Dain) 4
Baule (Côte d' Ivoire) 2
Beja (Kassala, Sudan; Ethiopia) 1
Bemba (Zambia) 2
Bengali[1]/(Bengal, India; Bangladesh) 184
Berber[2]
Beti (Cameroon; Gabon; Eq. Guinea) 2
Bhili (India) 3
Bikol (SE Luzon, Philippines) 4
Brahui (Pakistan; Afghanistan; Iran) 1
Bugis (Indonesia; Malaysia) 4
Bulgarian (Bulgaria) 9
Burmese (Burma) 30
Buyi (S Guizhou, S China) 2
Byelorussian (USSR) 10
Cantonese (or Yue) (China; Hong Kong) 63
Catalan (NE Spain; S France; Andorra) 9
Cebuano (Bohol Sea area, Philippines) 12
Chagga (Kilimanjaro area, Tanzania) 1
Chiga (Ankole, Uganda) 1
Chinese[3]
Chuvash (USSR) 2
Czech (Czechoslovakia) 12
Danish (Denmark) 5
Dimli (EC Turkey) 1
Dogri (Jammu-Kashmir, C and E India) 1
Dong (Guizhou, Hunan, Guangxi, China) 2
Dutch-Flemish (Netherlands; Belgium) 21
Dyerma (SW Niger) 2
Edo (Bendel, S Nigeria) 1
Efik (incl. Ibido) (SE Nigeria; W Cameroon) 6
English 443
Esperanto 2
Estonian (Estonia) 1
Ewe (SE Ghana; S Togo) 3

Fang-Bulu (Dialects of Beti, q.v.)
Farsi (Iranian form of Persian, q.v.)
Finnish (Finland; Sweden)   6
Flemish (see Dutch-Flemish)
Fon (SC Benin; S Togo)   1
French (France, Switzerland)   121
Fula (or Peulh) (Cameroon; Nigeria)   13
Fulakunda (Senegambia; Guinea Bissau)   2
Futa Jalon (NW Guinea; Sierra Leone)   3
Galician (Galicia, NW Spain)   3
Galla (see Oromo)
Ganda (or Luganda) (S Uganda)   3
Georgian (USSR)   4
German (Germany; Austria; Switzerland)   118
Gilaki (Gilan, NW Iran)   2
Gogo (Riff Valley, Tanzania)   1
Gondi (Central India)   2
Greek (Greece)   12
Guarani (Paraguay)   4
Gujarati (W and C India; S Pakistan)   38
Gusii (Kisii District, Nyanza, Kenya)   2
Hadiyya (Arusi, Ethiopia)   2
Hakka (or Kejia) (SE China)   32
Hani (S China)   1
Hausa (N Nigeria; Niger; Cameroon)   34
Haya (Kagera, NW Tanzania)   1
Hebrew (Israel)   4
Hindi[4]   352
Ho (Buhar and Orissa states, India)   1
Hungarian (or Magyar) (Hungary)   14
Iban (Kalimantan, Indonesia; Malaysia)   1
Ibidio (see Efik)
Igbo (or Ibo) (lower Niger R., Nigeria)   16
Ijaw (Niger River delta, Nigeria)   2
Ilocano (NW Luzon, Philippines)   7
Indonesian (see Malay-Indonesian)

Italian (Italy)	63
Japanese (Japan)	125
Javanese (Java, Indonesia)	58
Kabyle (W Kabylia, N Algeria)	3
Kamba (E Kenya)	3
Kannada[1] (S India)	3
Kanuri (Nigeria; Niger; Chad; Cameroon)	4
Karen (see Sgaw)	
Karo-Dairi (N Sumatra, Indonesia)	2
Kashmiri[1] (N India; NE Pakistan)	4
Kazakh (USSR)	8
Kenuzi-Dongola (S Egypt; Sudan)	1
Khalkha (see Mongolian)	
Khmer (Kampuchea; Vietnam; Thailand)	7
Khmer, Northern (Thailand)	1
Kikuyu (or Gekoyo) (W and C Kenya)	5
Kirghiz (USSR)	2
Kituba (Bas-Zaire, Bandundu, Zaire)	4
Kongo (W Zaire; S Congo; NW Angola)	3
Konkani (Maharashta and SW India)	4
Korean (North and South Korea; China; Japan) ...	71
Kurdish (south-west of Caspian Sea)	9
Kurukh (or Oraon) (C and E India)	2
Lampung (Sumatra, Indonesia)	1
Lao[5] (Laos)	4
Latvian (Latvia)	2
Lingala (incl. Bangala) (Zaire)	6
Lithuanian (Lithuania)	2
Luba-Lulua (or Chiluba) (Kasai, Zaire)	6
Luba-Shaba (Shaba, Zaire)	1
Lubu (E Sumatra, Indonesia)	1
Luhya (W Kenya)	3
Luo (Kenya; Nyanza, Tanzania)	3
Luri (SW Iran; Iraq)	3
Lwena (E Angola; W Zambia)	1
Macedonian (Macedonia, Yugoslavia)	2

Madurese (Madura, Indonesia)   10
Magindanaon (Moro, Gulf, S Philippines)   1
Makassar (S Sulawesi, Indonesia)   2
Makua (S Tanzania; N Mozambique)   3
Malagasy (Madagascar) 11
Malay-Indonesian 142
Malay, Pattani (SE pennisular Thailand)   1
Malayalam[1] (Kerala, India) 34
Malinke-Bambara-Dyula (W Africa)   9
Mandarin (China, Taiwan, Singapore)   864
Marathi[1] (Maharashtra, India) 64
Mazandarani (S Mazandaran, N Iran)   2
Mbundu (or Umbundu) (Benguela, Angola)   3
Mbundu (or Kimbundu) (Luanda Angola)   3
Meithei (NE India; Bangladesh)   1
Mende (S and E Sierra Leone)   2
Meru (Eastern Province, C Tanzania)   1
Miao (or Hmong) (S China; SE Asia)   5
Mien (China; Vietnam; Laos; Thailand)   2
Min (SE China; Taiwan; Malaysia)   48
Minangkabau (W Sumatra, Indonesia)   6
Moldavian (included with Romanian)
Mongolian (Mongolia; NE China)   5
Mordvin (USSR) 1
Moré (central part of Burkina Faso)   4
Nepali (Nepal, NE India; Bhutan)   13
Ngulu (Zambezia, Mozambique Malawi)   2
Nkole (Western Province, Uganda)   1
Norwegian (Norway) 5
Nung (NE of Hanoi, Vietnam; China)   1
Nupe (Kwara, Niger States, Nigeria)   1
Nyamwezi-Sukuma (NW Tanzania)   4
Nyanja (Malawi; Zambia; N Zimbabwe)   4
Oriya[1] (E India) 30
Oromo (W Ethiopia; N Kenya)   10
Pampangan (NW of Manila, Philippines)   2

Panay-Hiligaynon (Philippines)	6
Pangasinan (Philippines)	2
Pashtu (Pakistan; Afghanistan; Iran)	21
Pedi (see Sotho, Northern)	
Persian (Iran; Afghanistan)	32
Polish (Poland)	43
Portuguese (Portugal, Brazil)	173
Provençal (S France)	4
Punjabi[1] (Punjab, Pakistan; NW India)	84
Pushto (see Pashtu—many spellings)	
Quechua (Peru; Bolivia Ecuador; Argentina)	8
Rejang (SW Sumatra, Indonesia)	1
Riff (N Morocco; Algerian coast)	1
Romanian (Romania; Moldavia, USSR)	25
Romany (Vlach only) (Europe; America)	1
Ruanda (Rwanda; S Uganda; E Zaire)	8
Rundi (Burundi)	6
Russian (USSR)	293
Samar-Leyte (Central E Philippines)	3
Sango (Central African Republic)	3
Santali (E India; Nepal)	5
Sasak (Lombok, Alas Strait, Indonesia)	1
Serbo-Croatian (Yugoslavia)	20
Sgaw (SW, W, N of Rangoon, Burma)	1
Shan (Shan, E Burma)	3
Shilha (W Algeria; S Morocco)	3
Shona (Zimbabwe)	7
Sidamo (Sidamo, S Ethiopia)	1
Sindhi[1] (SE Pakistan; W India)	16
Sinhalese (Sri Lanka)	13
Slovak (Czechoslovakia)	5
Slovene (Slovenia, NW Yugoslavia)	2
Soga (Busoga, Uganda)	1
Somali (Somalia; Ethiopia; Kenya; Djibouti)	7
Songye (Kasia Or., NW Shala, Zaire)	1
Soninke (Mali; countries to W, S, E)	1

Sotho, Northern (South Africa) 3
Sotho, Southern (South Africa; Lesotho) 4
Spanish (Spain; Central and South America;
    Caribbean) 341
Sundanese (Sunda Strait, Indonesia) 24
Swahili (Kenya; Tanzania; Zaire; Uganda) 43
Swati (Swaziland; South Africa) 1
Swedish (Sweden; Finland) 9
Sylhetti (Bangladesh) 5
Tagalog (Philippines) 36
Tajiki (USSR) 4
Tamazight (N Morocco; W Algeria) 3
Tamil[1] (Tamil Nadu, India; Sri Lanka) 65
Tatar (USSR) 7
Tausug (Philippines; Malaysia) 1
Telugu[1] (Andhra Pradesh, SE India) 68
Temne (C Sierra Leone) 1
Thai[5] (Thailand) 48
Tho (N Vietnam; S China) 1
Thonga (Mozambique; South Africa) 3
Tibetan (SW China; N India; Nepal) 5
Tigrinya (S Eritrea, Tigre, Ethiopia) 4
Tiv (SE Nigeria; Cameroon) 2
Tong (see Dong)
Tonga (SW Zambia; NW Zimbabwe) 2
Tswana (Botswana; South Africa) 3
Tudza (N Vietnam; S China) 1
Tulu (S India) 2
Tumbuka (N Malawi; NE Zambia) 2
Turkish (Turkey) 55
Turkmen (S USSR; NE Iran; Afghanistan) 3
Twi-Fante (see Akan)
Uighur (Xinjang, NW China; SC USSR) 7
Ukrainian (USSR; Poland) 45
Urdu[4] (Pakistan; India) 92
Uzbek (USSR) 13

Vietnamese (Vietnam)	57
Wolaytta (SW Ethiopia)	2
Wolof (Senegal)	6
Wu (Shanghai and nearby provinces, China)	62
Xhosa (SW Cape Province, South Africa)	7
Yao (see Mien)	
Yao (Malawi; Tanzania; Mozambique)	
Yi (S and SW China)	6
Yiddish[6]	
Yoruba (SW Nigeria; Zou, Benin)	18
Zande (NE Zaire; SW Sudan)	1
Zhuang (S China)	14
Zulu (N Natal, South Africa; Lesotho)	7

(1) One of the fifteen languages of the Constitution of India. (2) See Kabyle, Riff, Shilha, and Tamazight. (3) See Mandarin, Cantonese, Wu, Min, and Hakka. The "common speech" (*Putonghua*) or the "national language" (*Guoyu*) is a standardized form of Mandarin as spoken in the area of Beijing. (4) Hindi and Urdu are essentially the same language, Hindustani. As the official language of Pakistan it is written in a modified Arabic script and called Urdu. As the official language of India it is written in the Devanagari script and called Hindi. (5) The distinctions between some Thai dialects and Lao is political rather than linguistic. (6) Yiddish is usually considered a variant of German, though it has its own standard grammar, dictionaries, a highly developed literature, and is written in Hebrew characters.

Farber's Language Reviews

We have such things as theater reviews, movie reviews, book reviews, and restaurant reviews to help trusting readers decide which plays, movies, books, and restaurants are worth their time and money.

So here is a series of language reviews—thumbnail sketches of some of the major languages of the world with comments on their prevalence, their usefulness, the difficulty or ease with which each may be learned, and special characteristics the potential learner should know.

French

After English, French is the world's most popular second language. Several other languages are spoken by more people: Chinese, English, Hindustani (the spoken form of Hindi and Urdu), Russian, Spanish, Japanese, German, Indonesian, and even Portuguese count more speakers than French. But French can be heard in virtually every corner of the word and is often spoken by the most influential segments of a given population. The old French empire, though not as vast as the British, was nonetheless vast. French is therefore spoken in what you may find a surprising number of countries. So is Chinese, but the French spoken by the educated classes and government officials in Canada, Africa, Lebanon and throughout the Middle East, Asia, the Caribbean, and the South Pacific outweighs in cultural influence the Chinese spoken in the Chinatowns of America, Indonesia, the Philippines, Singapore, Burma, Vietnam, London, and everywhere else.

French no longer deserves its reputation as "the language of diplomacy" (during how many summit meetings since World War II have the chiefs of state been able to communicate even one simple thought to each other in French?), but never mind. French is still respected and revered as a language of cultured people the world over.

Fully sixty percent of all those who come to practice parties at the Language Club in New York come seeking practice in French. Efforts to convince Americans shopping around for a language to learn to shift their attentions from French to currently more advantageous languages like Japanese, Chinese, Russian, and Arabic are usually unavailing. It's French they want!

French lies in the middle range of difficulty to learn. The grammar is mercifully simple, but correct pronunciation with a decent French accent is hard to achieve. And for some reason, bad French comes across as much worse than bad German, bad Italian, bad Spanish, or bad anything else. The native French ear and French attitude are unforgiving.

There are no noun cases, but verbs inflect and adjectives must agree with nouns. There's a subjunctive mood you're strongly urged to learn even though the younger French themselves increasingly ignore it.

If you're planning to study French along with other languages, make sure you learn French best of all. You will be judged in the world by your French, and no matter how well you handle Dutch, Hungarian, Norwegian, or Indonesian, you will not be regarded as a person of language accomplishment if your French is poor.

Spanish

Spanish seems to be the "natural" second language for Americans, owing to our proximity to the Spanish-speaking centers of North, Central, and South America and the growing prevalence of Spanish in our country. It's easier for Americans to speak good Spanish than good French. It's a more phonetic language and you don't have the problem of the last few letters of a word being silent—as you often do in French. Also, correct Spanish pronunciation is less difficult than correct French pronunciation.

Spanish grammar is similar to French (as is that of all other Romance languages), and the subjunctive tense waits to test your character.

There are some happy surprises in store for Spanish learners. Of course you expect Spanish to carry you through Latin America and Spain, but you may not expect to be able to communicate with the older generation in the Philippines and even with Sephardic Jews in Israel (as well as Greece, Turkey, Yugoslavia, and Bulgaria) whose vernacular is a language known as Ladino, a fifteenth- and sixteenth-century Spanish with a Hebrew admixture that is written in the Hebrew alphabet. Spanish offers perhaps the grandest of good-deal opportunities. Whoever learns Spanish holds an option to acquire Portuguese at half price.

Portuguese

Don't dismiss Portuguese as some kind of slurring, overnasalized cousin of Spanish.

The lightning population growth of Portuguese-speaking Brazil alone makes Portuguese a major world language. Ancient Portuguese navigators carried the language to the mid-Atlantic, the African countries of Angola and Mozambique, the enclave of Goa in India, and even the Indonesian island of Timor.

Portuguese is the ninth most-widely spoken language in the world, after Chinese, English, Hindi-Urdu, Russian, Spanish, Japanese, German, and Indonesian. Thus, Portuguese is an intelligent choice for the language "shopper" who wants to be different without abandoning the mainstream.

Portuguese nasal sounds are easier than the French and the grammar is only slightly more difficult than Spanish. Because I learned Spanish first, Portuguese will always sound to me like Spanish that's been damaged on delivery. (That's just a smile, not an insult. Dutch sounds the same way to anyone who's first studied German, Danish sounds that way to anyone who's first studied Norwegian, and Serbo-Croatian definitely fits the description to anyone who's first studied Russian.)

German

Germany didn't leave us a world of colonies where people still speak German, but they may as well have. In addition to being the principal language of Germany, Austria, and one of the three main languages of Switzerland, German is, surprisingly, the language most natives will try first on foreigners when they come visiting in Hungary, Yugoslavia, Czechoslovakia, Poland, Latvia, Lithuania, Estonia—in fact all the way from Germany's eastern boarder with Poland as far east as Moscow and from the Baltic Sea in the north clear down to the Mediterranean. English may edge German out by the time of the next scientific poll in Eastern Europe, but that leaves a tremendous number of German speakers across Europe and elsewhere. Germany's reunification, reestablishing Germany as the central European power, can only intensify the German language's importance.

German grammar is far from the most difficult, though you'll be hard to convince when you find yourself trapped in one of German's unending dependent clauses. You can wait through lunch for the German noun after a loop-the-loop adjectival clause that might translate literally as "the never- having- defin-

itively- researched- the- mating- habits- of- the- Asian- armadil-
lo Dr. Schultz," and you can wait even longer for the German
verb. It's something you get the hang of, though, and remember, German is family. Its kinship with English will be a boon
throughout.

There are three genders in German and officially four noun
cases, but they're easy. In only one case does the noun itself
change endings, the rest being taken care of by the preceding
article, adjective, or other modifier.

German offers dividends to those interested in science, phi-
losophy, opera, and getting a good job in international commerce.

Italian

Everybody who's ever wrestled with Latin deserves to pick up
an Italian grammar book just to relax. Italian is easy Latin, a
delight to plunge into. There are three different types of verbs,
but noun cases have been eliminated. Unlike French, Italian
pronunciation is church-bell clear, and you can read Italian off
the page and be understood after mastering the regular rules
governing the sounds of the letters. There are no orthographical booby traps such as the English *tough, weigh, night, though,*
and the dozens of other deceptive spellings we Americans can
be grateful we never had to learn as foreigners.

Opera, art, wine, cuisine, history, and archaeology are some
of the motivators for learning Italian. Italians are nicer to foreigners trying to learn their language than any other people
whose language is a major one. A passable attempt to speak
French in France is likely to bring little but grudging comprehension from the French. A passable attempt to speak Italian in
Italy will likely lead to an explosive exclamation, "Ahh, you
speak our language!" followed by an offer of a free espresso.

Dutch

It's easy to dismiss Dutch as a slim shadow of its big language
neighbor, German, and of possible interest only to those

Americans eager to ingratiate themselves with an aging aunt in Amsterdam with a valuable art collection. Not so fast. In addition to the Dutch spoken in Holland, there are millions of Belgians whose language may be officially called Flemish but is actually nothing but Dutch going under an assumed name. You've also got millions of educated Indonesians who speak Dutch as a historical echo from the four hundred years of Dutch colonial rule. Moreover, Dutch is the mother tongue of Afrikaans, the language of those white South Africans whose ancestors were the Boers (*boer* is the Dutch word for "farmer"). Afrikaaners not only understand Dutch but look up to Dutch much as an Alabaman looks up to someone who speaks British English.

Dutch is much simpler for Americans to learn than German. There are only two genders (oddly enough, not masculine and feminine, but common and neuter). Verb endings don't change as much in Dutch as in German, and its word order is more like English than German's is.

You need not pretend Dutch is a beautiful language. The Dutch themselves joke about the coarseness of their language. It's got more of a guttural sound than Arabic, Hebrew, Russian, and Persian. If you want a concert in Dutch guttural, ask the next person who speaks Dutch to say, *"Misschien is Uw scheermesje niet scherp genoeg."* It means "Perhaps your razor blade is not sharp enough," but that's irrelevant. That short sentence explodes with five gutturals that cause the speaker to sound like the exhaust pipe of a Greyhound bus through a full set of gear changes!

When you learn Dutch, you can cash in on at least forty-percent credit when you decide to take up German.

Russian

Russian is the world's fourth language in number of speakers after Chinese, English, and Hindustani. It is extremely difficult to learn to speak Russian correctly, but the Russians have learned to be patient with foreigners who speak incorrect Russian. Journalists and others fascinated by discussing recent history with Soviet citizens suddenly free to talk to foreigners get a lot of joy out of knowing Russian. The much-touted commercial advantages of learning Russian, however, have so far fallen far short of expectation.

The jobs with gargantuan salaries promised to Russian speakers as a fruit of the resurgence of free enterprise in the Soviet Union are few and shaky as the early enthusiasm of foreign investors gives way to wait-and-see attitudes. Long range, Russian remains a good bet for those willing to learn a language for career advantage. And in the meantime you can enjoy reading Chekhov and Dostoyevski in the original.

The Russian alphabet may look formidable, but it's a false alarm. It can be learned in twenty minutes, but then you've got to face the real obstacles, such as three genders; six noun cases with wave upon wave of noun groups that decline differently; a past tense that behaves like an adjective; and verbs that have not just person, number, and tense, but also something called "aspect"—perfective or imperfective.

Knowing Russian yields a lot of satisfaction. You want to pinch yourself as you find yourself gliding through a printed page of a language you may have grown up suspecting and fearing. Russian, like German, crackles with good, gutsy sounds that please you as they leap from your tongue. Russian is a high-gratitude language. The new immigrants from the Soviet Union, though they speak one of the major languages of the world, don't expect Americans to know it. They'll be overjoyed to hear their language from you.

One advantage of choosing Russian is the head start it offers in almost a dozen other Slavic languages, should you suddenly want or need one.

Chinese

Chinese is actually more of a life involvement than a language you choose to study. When you're in your easy chair studying, Chinese has more power to make you forget it's dinner time than any other language. It has more power to draw you out of bed earlier than necessary to sneak in a few more moments of study. There's simply more there.

More people speak Chinese than any other language on earth. There's hardly a community in the world that doesn't have someone who speaks Chinese as a native. Even in the 1940s, when I first began studying Chinese, there was a Chinese restaurant and a Chinese laundry in our small town of Greensboro, North Carolina. You can count on conversation practice in Chinese from the Chinese laundries of Costa Rica to the Chinese restaurants of Israel.

The Chinese Communists on the mainland and the Chinese Nationalists on Taiwan agree that the national language of Chinese is the northern Chinese dialect of Mandarin. Accept no substitute. Be sure you know what you're doing if you set out to learn any Chinese dialect other than Mandarin! It was almost impossible to find a Chinese in a Chinese restaurant in America who spoke Mandarin forty years ago. They all spoke a subdialect of Cantonese, being descendants of the Chinese laborers who came to build America's transcontinental railroad in the 1800s. Today it's almost impossible to find a Chinese restaurant in America where the waiters *don't* speak Mandarin.

Don't let yourself get drawn into Cantonese merely because your Chinese friends happen to be of Cantonese descent or because your new employees are from Cantonese-speaking Hong Kong. Even the Cantonese themselves are now trying to learn Mandarin!

Spoken Chinese is enthrallingly easy. There's nothing we could call "grammar" in Chinese. Verbs, nouns, and adjectives never change endings for any reason. I once caught a show-off student of Chinese trying to intimidate new students by warning them that Chinese had a different word for "yes" and "no" for each question! That's largely true, but not the slightest bit difficult.

The closest thing Chinese has to what we think of as grammar is what we'll call "interesting ways." When you pose a question in Chinese you present both alternatives. Thus, "Are you going?" becomes "You go not go?" or "Are you going or not?" If you *are* going, the word for "yes" to that question is "go." If you're not going, you say, "Not go." Likewise, "Are you going to play?" becomes, literally translated, "You play not play?" To answer "yes," you say "Play." "No" is "Not play."

You've already learned some of the "middle language" essential to the mastery of Chinese. Don't fear that, because there's a middle language, you're being called upon to learn two languages to acquire just one! It's a shortcut. The middle language is *English*—the way a Chinese would say it if all he could do were to come up with the English words literally and nothing more. Thus, "Do you have my pencil?" in middle language is "You have I-belong pencil, no have?" "The man who lives in the white house" becomes "Live in white house-belong man."

I find it helpful to look for the middle language no matter what language I'm studying. In Russian, "The vase is on the table" becomes "Vase on table." "Do you have a pen?" becomes "Is by you pen?" "I like the cake" in Spanish is "To me is pleasing the cake." "Where have you studied German?" in German is "Where have you German studied?" "Do you want me to help?" in Yiddish is "Do you want I should help?"—a construction that should come as no surprise to anyone with immigrant Jewish grandparents.

The middle language helps you get the hang of things. Once you see the structure as revealed by the middle language, it's easier for you to climb inside the target language. Learning the "interesting ways" through middle language is especially important in Chinese.

Chinese has no alphabet. Each ideogram or *character* is complete unto itself and each must be learned. There are said to be as many as fifty thousand Chinese characters. Fear not. You can carry on fairly sophisticated conversations with knowledge of a few hundred characters and you can carry on like a Ming orator once you compile a couple of thousand. You can read a

Chinese newspaper with fewer than six thousand. Though lacking an alphabet, Chinese nonetheless has 214 *radicals,* the elements that make up the building blocks for almost every Chinese character. The fact that there are clusters of Chinese characters that surrender to you by the family group makes the going quicker and easier.

One problem: the pronunciation of each Chinese character is always one syllable and one syllable only. Therefore, the same sound has to represent a lot of different things. We have a slight touch of that in English—a *pier* has nothing to do with a *peer*—but imagine how much utterance duplication you'd have if each word in the language were limited to one syllable only. (Beginners who learn that the Chinese word for "chopsticks" is *kwai dze* and "bus" is *gung gung chee chuh* may object. I simply mean that the term for "chopsticks" is two separate words [characters] in Chinese and the term for "bus" is four!) A Chinese textbook for Americans that makes no pretense of being complete lists seventy-five different meanings for the sound *shih* alone!

Chinese differentiates among the various possibilities of meaning by use of *tones.* Each Chinese word is assigned a specific tone, like a musical note. Mandarin Chinese has four tones, Cantonese has nine.

The word *wu* in Mandarin's first tone means "room," in tone two it means "vulgar," in tone three it means "five," and in tone four *wu* means "disobedient."

Take the sentence "Mother is scolding the horse." The spoken Chinese transliterates as *mā mà mà mǎ*. If we want to make it a question and ask "Is mother scolding the horse?" just add a fifth *ma*. Without the tones a Chinese would hear an unintelligible babble. With the correct tones, however, it would be as clear to him as "Peering at a pair of pears on the pier" is to us.

Ideally you should know the tone of each word and the circumstances under which words shift tones, but until you attain that lofty peak, you'll be okay if you do your best to imitate the tonality of the native Chinese speaker on your cassettes.

Much is made of our ability to read the Chinese soul through the Chinese language. "Tomorrow" in Chinese is *ming t'ien,* which literally means "bright day." The character for "good" literally depicts woman with a child, suggesting that a mother and child are emblematic of everything good. The character meaning "peace" depicts a woman under a roof.

All that is indeed fun but hardly a cryptanalysis of the Chinese soul. After all, how much can you tell about the English soul by noting that the word *breakfast* really means the "breaking" of the "fast" you've engaged in since your last bite the night before?

Japanese

Like Chinese, Japanese conversation is fairly easy, but the written language is complicated. In wartime, America turned out interpreters in Japanese and Chinese at a satisfactory rate by going straight for the spoken language and ignoring the written language completely. You may be tempted to do the same.

Certainly you can prioritize the ability to speak and understand over the ability to read and write, but I urge you to undertake serious study of the written language and continue steadily. If speech is to be your "hare," let writing be at least your "tortoise."

Written Japanese is not as difficult as you might fear. Japanese uses several thousand characters borrowed from the Chinese, but it uses them in a different and more limited way that makes them easy to learn. The characters are used along with two *syllabaries,* sets of simple written symbols, each of which represents not one single letter but a complete syllable.

Japanese has no tones to worry about, and Japanese grammar involves the learning of certain speech *patterns* more than changes in verbs, nouns, and adjectives.

Japanese has a clarity missing from Chinese. Learn a Japanese word from your book or cassette and your Japanese friend will understand it at your first attempt to use it.

The commercial advantages of learning Japanese are obvious and on the rise. But even if your Japanese never reaches a level of proficiency enabling you to do business in Japanese, your Japanese hosts and associates will appreciate your efforts. They, after all, *had* to learn English. You did not have to learn Japanese. Yet.

Arabic

Arabic is elusive, guttural, and rewarding. Arabic script, written from right to left, writes each letter differently depending upon whether it occurs at the beginning, the middle, or the end of a word. Learn it, however, and you'll be welcome from the North Atlantic coast of Africa clear through the Middle East to the borders of Iran and Pakistan. Arabic is also the religious language studied by millions of Muslims around the world whose native languages are not Arabic. The Arab population of the United States is growing rapidly. You can hear Arabic on the streets and deal in Arabic in the shops of places like Dearborn, Michigan, where there is a substantial Arab population.

Your investment in Arabic is likely to gain in value when Israel and the Arab states achieve a settlement allowing for commerce and development to replace a half-century of open warfare.

Hebrew

Hebrew is one of the more difficult languages, and the numerical incentives for tackling it are not great because Hebrew is spoken only in Israel and in small communities of Israelis in America and other western countries. Until recently the teaching of Hebrew was illegal in the Soviet Union, but classrooms are overflowing now across the country as Jews prepare to emigrate to Israel or assert their Jewishness inside the Soviet Union. Hebrew is spoken wherever Jews worship around the world, and there is a surge of interest in learning Hebrew among young Americans who were born Jewish even though they may not have had a strong Jewish upbringing.

If you're not Jewish and choose to learn Hebrew anyhow, you will set loose waves of appreciation among Jews grateful to outsiders willing to go to that much trouble.

Once you learn the Hebrew alphabet, you'll be in command of virtually the same alphabet used by Yiddish, a language based on fifteenth-century low German that was spoken by millions of East European Jews before Hitler's extermination and is still understood in a surprising number of places. It's also the alphabet used by Ladino, the "Spanish of Cervantes" that became the "Yiddish" of the Jews of Spanish origin who scattered throughout the eastern Mediterranean after the beginning of the Spanish Inquisition. There are few language thrills that can match that of an American who learned the Hebrew alphabet in Hebrew school looking at a printed page in a language he didn't know existed (many Jews themselves are totally unaware of the existence of Ladino) and discovering he can read it and understand it with his high-school Spanish!

Greek

Modern Greek has a grammar slightly less glorious than that of its ancient civilization. In difficulty, Greek falls somewhere between French and Russian. Each verb has two forms and verbs change according to person, number, and tense. The future tense is almost as easy as it is in English—the word *tha* serving the role of our *will*. Adjectives agree with their nouns according to gender (three of them) and number.

Greek enjoys a leftover prestige, not only from ancient times but from the not-long-vanished tradition of the scholar who prided himself on being at home in Latin and Ancient Greek. Every five minutes during your study of Greek you'll be reminded of our debt to the Greek language. *Zestos* means "hot" ("zesty"), *chronos* means "time" or "year," "number" is *arithmo,* when you want your check in a restaurant you ask for the *logariazmo* (as in "logarithm"), the Greek word for "clear" describing weather is *katharos* (as in "catharsis"), "season" is *epohi* ("epoch"), and so on.

Greek may be the language of one small European country only, but there are thriving Greek communities throughout the Middle East, Egypt and other parts of Africa, and the United States. Enterprising Greeks have carried the language around the world.

Swedish, Danish, Norwegian

The Scandinavian languages are lumped together because of their similarity and the reliability with which natives of one Scandinavian country can deal with the languages of the others. That similarity is something for you to know and enjoy, not something for you to mention to the Scandinavians themselves. They're horrified when outsiders say, "Gee, Swedish, Danish, and Norwegian are all alike!" They prefer to dwell upon the differences. There was a popular movement in Norwegian early in the twentieth century to change the language for no apparent reason other than to make it less like Danish.

If your aim is to communicate in all three countries, learn Norwegian first. It's the linguistic center of Scandinavia. A Dane can deal comfortably with Norwegian, but much less so with Swedish. A Swede can deal comfortably with Norwegian, but much less so with Danish. A Norwegian can deal comfortably with both Swedish and Danish.

The Scandinavian languages are relatively easy for Americans to learn. They're Germanic languages, related to English, but vastly easier to learn than German. The verbs don't change for person and number, and only slightly for tense. The word order follows English obligingly most of the way. Like Dutch, the Scandinavian languages have two genders—common and neuter—and the definite article follows the noun and becomes one word. (For example, "a pen" in Norwegian is *en penn*, "the pen" is *pennen*.)

Holland is said to be the non-English-speaking country with the highest percentage of people fluent in English. The three Scandinavian countries are close behind. You may never need their language no matter where you go or who you deal with in Scandinavia, but Scandinavians are among the most apprecia-tive people on earth if you know their language anyhow.

Polish, Croatian, Czech, Slovak, Slovenian

These western Slavic languages use the Roman alphabet. The eastern Slavic languages use the Cyrillic (sometimes mistaken-ly called the Russian) alphabet. Don't suggest it after a few drinks in Warsaw, but Polish might be better off using the Cyrillic alphabet. A Polish sound resembling the *sh* combined with the following *ch* in *push-charlie* is spelled *szcz* in Polish. That sound, which requires four letters in the Roman alphabet, needs only one in the Cyrillic! Romanizing Slavic languages leads to orthographical madness. A newspaper reporter in a small Southern town went into his editor's office and said, "There's been an earthquake in the Polish city of Pszczyna." He showed the editor the story off the wire. After a momentary frown the editor looked up and said, "Find out what the name of the place was before the earthquake!"

Except for Polish, none of these languages has much bounce beyond its borders, but if your reason for wanting to learn them involves family, love, or business, that won't matter. All Slavic languages are grammatically complex. Verbs change for rea-sons that leave even those who speak Romance languages weeping over their wine and wondering why. There are at least six noun cases in every Slavic language, sometimes seven.

The big payoff in learning any of these Slavic languages is the automatic down payment you're making on Russian itself. Russian will be a breeze if you already know another Slavic language, and conversely, the other Slavic languages will come more easily if you already know Russian.

Serbian, Bulgarian, Macedonian, Ukrainian, Byelorussian

Everything stated above about the western Slavic languages applies to these eastern Slavic languages with one exception—they use the Cyrillic alphabet, with slight variations from language to language.

The similarities between Serbian and Croatian, the main languages of Yugoslavia, are so striking the languages are usually lumped together as Serbo-Croatian.

If you know any two Slavic languages, you can make yourself understood in any of the other Slavic languages. That may be challenged by Slavic scholars, but it works well in real life between the western border of Poland and the Ural Mountains and from the arctic tip of Russia to the Black Sea beaches of Bulgaria.

Indonesian

Indonesia is the world's most populous Muslim nation. Consisting of hundreds of islands spread out over a south Pacific area the size of the United States, Indonesia is easily the largest country in the world about which the most other people in the world know the least. With enough mineral wealth in the ground to make it an economic superpower, Indonesia is still frequently confused with India or Polynesia.

Indonesian is the easiest major language in the world for a foreigner to learn. It was called *Pasar Malay* ("Bazaar Malay") by the colonial Dutch who looked upon the Indonesian language as a kind of baby talk for servants and merchants. When Indonesia won independence in 1948, the ruler, Sukarno, did his best to take that unstructured language and graft some sophisticated grammar onto it to make it more regimented and thus difficult. He failed.

Indonesian still has nothing that will be regarded as grammar by anybody who's done battle with Latin or Russian. There are suffixes and prefixes aplenty, neat and regular, that convert verbs into nouns and give verbs additional meanings and the like, but no inflections according to person, number, tense, aspect, or anything else.

Indonesian uses the Roman alphabet and is delightfully easy to pronounce. If you've ever studied any other language, you'll marvel at how quickly and clearly you'll understand and be understood.

Indonesian is closely related to Malayan, the language of Malaysia and Singapore, and gives you a head start in Tagalog, the major language of the Philippines.

Hindi and Urdu

The spoken languages of India and Pakistan, Hindi and Urdu, are so close that the true language-lover is tempted to take the plunge even though both languages use different and, to us, unfamiliar scripts (Devanagari, and a mixture of Persian and Arabic). Though other languages abound on the Indian sub-continent, Hindi-Urdu united their respective nations and whoever jumps in (despite the current lack of good learning materials) will be able to communicate with a population second only to that of China.

Hungarian, Finnish, Estonian

Despite the grammatical complexity and the relatively small pool of native speakers, an occasional adventurer is drawn almost masochistically to the three Finno-Ugric languages. If you were the hated kid in ninth grade who stayed after algebra class to beg the teacher to introduce you to calculus, you might want to try one of these.

Every word in all three languages is accented on the first syllable—every single word, names and all, giving those languages the sound of a pneumatic jackhammer breaking up a sidewalk. There are, in Finnish, fifteen noun cases in the singular and sixteen in the plural. Hungarian and Estonian aren't far behind. And that's the easy part!

People whose language you choose to learn often ask polite questions about why you wanted to learn their language. Let on to a Finn, a Hungarian, or an Estonian that you know a little bit of *their* language and you will not be merely questioned. You'll be cross-examined!

Swahili

Swahili enjoyed a surge of support beginning in the late 1960s among young American blacks who wanted to reconnect to their African roots. Anyone who pressed on and mastered Swahili would today speak a language spoken by fifty million people living in central and eastern Africa, including the nations of Kenya and Tanzania in which Swahili is the national language. Swahili is a Bantu language, and once you learn it you can expect easy going when you decide to learn Kiganda, Kikamba, Kikuyu, Kinyanja, Kichaga, Kiluba, Kishona, Kizulu, Kikongo, and Kiduala, all of which are spoken over smaller areas in Africa south of the Sahara.

Swahili uses the Roman alphabet. The *Say It in Swahili* phrase book advises us not to be discouraged by words like *kitakachonisahilishia,* because Swahili grammar is mercifully regular and logical!

English

The mere fact that you're reading these words right now calls for self-congratulations. It means you're fluent in the winner, the international language, the number-one language of all time!

When a Soviet plane approaches the airport in China, the pilot and the control tower don't speak Russian to each other.

They don't speak Chinese. They speak English. If an Italian plane is about to land in another part of Italy, the Italian pilot and the Italian traffic control person also speak English.

When the Israeli general and the Egyptian general met in Sinai in October 1973 to talk truce in the Yom Kippur War, they didn't speak Hebrew. They didn't speak Arabic. They spoke English.

When Norwegian whaling ships put in to the port of Capetown, South Africa, to hire Zulu seamen, the interviewing is not done in Norwegian or Zulu. It's done in English.

The parliaments of Sweden, Denmark, and Norway send delegates to a body called the Nordic Council. Their official meetings are conducted—at great expense in interpreters and simultaneous interpretation equipment—in Swedish, Danish, and Norwegian. When the meetings end, however, and the delegates from the three neighboring countries adjourn to the bar and the dining room, they all start speaking English with each other!

Haven't you noticed something odd about protesters you have seen on TV demonstrating in Lithuania, Estonia, Korea, Iraq, Mexico, and other countries where neither the protestors, the ones they're protesting against, nor the local media speak native English? In addition to the signs and banners in their own languages, they always carry signs and banners in English. And for good reason. They want their message to reverberate around the world.

On a map of Africa, Nigeria seems a tiny patch where the bulge of that gigantic continent meets the body. Inside that patch, however, live between 100 and 120 million people speaking 250 different languages, with names like Yoruba, Ibo, Hausa, Nupe, and Oyo. From their first day of school, the children of Nigeria are taught English. Without English, not only could Nigeria not talk to the world, Nigerians couldn't even talk to each other.

When a Nigerian educator, Aliu Babtunde Fafunwa, proposed in early 1991 that Nigerian children begin their education in their respective 250 mother tongues, the government newspaper itself wrote in an editorial, "The least luxury we can afford in the last decade of the twentieth century is an idealistic experiment in linguistic nationalism which could cut our children off from the main current of human development." That's hardly a hate-filled denunciation of former colonial masters.

Every attempt to launch an artificial international language has so far failed. Esperanto, Idiom Neutral, Kosmos, Monoglottica, Universalsprache, Neo-Latine, Vertparl, Mundolingue, Dil, Volapuk, even an international language based on the notes of the music scale, all started out weak and gradually tapered off. My guess is they always will. You no more "vote" a language into being *the* international language than you can vote warmth into a blizzard.

Languages attain prominence something the way individuals and countries do, through all kinds of force, including war. There's an added element in language prominence, however. Brute force is not enough. The winning language must have a degree of acceptability to the losers.

Russian emerged from World War II as a mighty language, but it failed to bluster beyond the bounds of the Communist empire. Russian even failed to inspire people to learn it *inside* their empire. Students in Hungary, Romania, and East Germany knew no more Russian after eight years of schooling than Americans know French after similar exposure.

English, on the other hand, was welcomed. Africans and Asians may not have rejoiced at being forcibly incorporated into the British Empire, but they recognized that the English language, if learned by all, was a unifying tool that enabled different tribes who lived five miles apart to communicate for the first time, in a language brought down upon them from thousands of miles away.

A wolf will lift his neck to let a larger wolf know that he accepts the other's dominant role as leader. The entire world has lifted its neck to acknowledge English as the language of choice in the modern world. It wasn't all military and commercial power, either. American movies, songs, comic strips, TV series, even T-shirts all helped make English the international language of the earth by acclaim.

But only the shortsighted will consider the dominance of English reason to return foreign language materials to the bookstore and forget the whole thing. It's precisely because the peoples of the world honor our language that we get so much more appreciation when we nonetheless go out of our way to honor theirs.